Hasan Shah's

THE NAUTCH GIRL
A Novel

Two hundred years ago, in 1790, Hasan Shah, a young man of Kanpur wrote his autobiographical novel *Nashtar* (Surgeon's Knife). The conventional literary meaning of *nashtar* implied the excruciating pain of love and separation from one's beloved—in this case, Khanum Jan, the remarkable heroine of the novel. She belonged to a band of camp followers who sang and danced for English officers of the East India Company stationed at the cantonments of Oudh in north India. *Nashtar* was written in 'Hindi-ised Farsi', as Persian was one of the generally used Indian languages at that time. The novel was rendered into Urdu in 1899.

The Jnanpith Award-winning Urdu novelist, Qurratulain Hyder, has abridged and translated *Nashtar* into English, adhering strictly to the Urdu-Persian text. The title has been changed to *Nautch Girl*, which is more to the point for the present day reader. The technique and style, and the realistic portrayal of the contemporary social scene in the author's time make *Nashtar* or *Nautch Girl* India's first modern novel, as discovered by the present translator.

Qurratulain Hyder is a trend setter in modern Urdu fiction. She has published several novels, novellas, collections of short stories and reportages. She has received India's highest literary honour, the Jnanpith Award (1989), the Sahitya Akademi Award (1967), and Padmashri (1984).

Qurratulian Hyder is an academic as well as a journalist. She was Managing Editor of the magazine Imprint, *Bombay (1964-68) and a member of the editorial staff of the* Illustrated Weekly of India *(1968-75). Currently, she is Professor, Khan Abdul Ghaffar Khan Chair, Jamia Millia Islamia, New Delhi.*

Published by
Sterling Publishers Private Limited

Hasan Shah's
THE NAUTCH GIRL
A Novel

translated by
QURRATULAIN HYDER

A Sterling Paperback

STERLING PAPERBACKS
An imprint of
Sterling Publishers (P) Ltd.
L-10, Green Park Extension, New Delhi-110016

The Nautch Girl: A Novel
©1992, Qurratulain Hyder
ISBN 81 207 1388 5

All rights are reserved. No part of this publication may be reproduced, stored in a retrieval system or transmitted, in any form or by any means, mechanical, photocopying, recording or otherwise, without prior written permission of the publisher.

Published by Sterling Publishers Pvt. Ltd.,
L-10, Green Park Extn., New Delhi-110016.
Printed at Print India, Mayapuri, New Delhi.
Cover Printed at Crescent Printing Press, New Delhi
Cover design by Biplab

Foreword

It is generally believed that novel-writing began in Victorian India and that this genre was imported from England. However, *Nashtar* was written by Hasan Shah, a young man of Kanpur, as far back as 1790, which makes it the first known modern Indian novel.

Many historians of Urdu fiction are familiar with the Urdu version of *Nashtar* but the present translator's research reveals an astounding fact: Hasan Shah wrote this original story uninfluenced by English novels. He portrayed his contemporary English nabob-and-the-nautch girl scene in an effective, realistic manner with very few lapses into the old *dastan* style.

The novel was written in Persian, at a time when Raja Ram Mohun Roy was also writing his books in that language (Persian was officially replaced by English in 1836). *Nashtar* (Surgeon's Knife) signified excruciating pain of separation from one's beloved. It is the story of a dancing girl, Khanum Jan, who has to entertain, albeit reluctantly, the English officers of East India Company. The narrator falls in love with her and marries her. The novel ends in tragedy. Because the heroine is a dancer, I have taken the liberty of changing the title from *Nashtar* to *The Nautch Girl* which is more to the point.

Nashtar was translated by Sajjad Hussain Kasmandavi into Urdu and serialised in the famous journal *Oudh Punch*. In 1893, it was published from Lucknow as a slim volume of 155 pages. The Persian book is extinct. I have translated Kasmandavi's edition. It is obvious that he has remained extremely faithful to the original and retains many passages and all Persian ghazals in his text. From time to time he makes his humorous comments on the author's views and actions.

Kasmandavi says in his preface that he is presenting, in Urdu, a true story written in simple "Hindi-ised Persian" language. "The details about this book require a comprehensive introduction," he adds, "but I cannot do so at the moment; nobody would take the trouble of reading it. The book was written in 1205 A.H. (1790 A.D.)."

In his own foreword, author Syed Hasan Shah, introduces himself (in the usual courtly manner) as a clerk (munshi) who worked for an English officer called Ming. (Both "Ming" and "Kallan Saheb" may have been Manning and Collins, just as Warren Hastings had been turned into Hastan Bahadur, Colonel Skinner was called Sikander Saheb.)

Hasan Shah further informs us that Ming was a nephew of Sir Eyre Coote. He was stationed at Cawnpore which had been an English cantonment from the time of the Rohilla Wars. (The famous Gen. Eyre Coote was Commander-in-Chief in India and a member of the Supreme Council. He defeated Hyder Ali at Porto Novo in 1781 and died in Madras in 1783.) At the time of the writing of this novel the British had gained political supremacy in India. The Battles of Buxar and Kora Jehanabad had been fought and won. According to a treaty signed by Nawab Asaf-ud-Dowlah, Oudh had to pay a heavy subsidy to East India Company in order to maintain their garrisons at Cawnpore, Farrukhabad, and Chunargarh (near Benaras).

The British had destroyed Indian economy. Individually they had amassed great wealth and adopted the lifestyle of Indian aristocracy. In England they were being called "the Nabobs". They took Indian mistresses, or married Indian girls of good families. The custom of maintaining a harem or zenana became more popular after 1760.

According to Professor Percival Spear, "Engaging troops of dancing girls had become common practice for the English in India. It was their chief amusement, along with riding, hunting, shooting." About "The European addiction to nautch," Spear writes: "Soon enough as ladies arrived in India to make European dancing practicable, the whole community took to it with enthusiasm. But they retained their taste for the nautch. To see a nautch was something like attending the ballet in Europe, with the difference that the troop always came to a private house; in the transition period it was the substitute for the theatre....The European taste for a nautch is further shown by the fact that it became the recognised form of entertainment for an Indian merchant to provide for his English guests. As so easily happens in India, it became traditional, and continued long after the European taste itself had disappeared. 'When a black man has a mind, to compliment a European, he treats him to a nautch,' wrote Mrs. Kindersley in 1754, and the custom still existed at the time of Mrs. Fenton's visit to Calcutta in 1826.

"During the transition period its popularity continued unchecked, and though some had doubts of its propriety, all acknowledged its charm. 'It is their languishing glances, wanton smiles, and attitudes not quite consistent with decency, which are so much admired,' wrote Mrs. Kindersley. Hart in 1775 speaks of 'six or seven black girls being brought in after dinner' when 'they sang and danced well', and in 1778 they were still 'much admired by the European gentlemen'.

"In the army enthusiasm for the nautch continued till the end of the century, perhaps because of the lack of facilities for European dancing. According to Sir J. D'Oyley, 'the influx of officers from 1778 led to the best sets going to the cantonments' until 'reason rode past on the wings of military retrenchment, and the Auditor General's red ink negatives dissolved the charm'. The taste nevertheless continued, and at the different camping grounds the officers would be entertained by sets from the neighbouring village or pagoda."

After the Fall of Delhi (1757) the dance groups had spread out to other regions seeking employment. Some of the dancing girls belonged originally to the gypsy tribes of Punjab and Sind. Many were Kashmiris. They were highly appreciated because of their exceptional good looks.

The Kashmiris were mostly seasonal migrants who came down to the planes to sell their shawls. Many settled down in cities like Lucknow and Delhi. (One family in Lucknow still lives in the same old mansion from where its ancestors exported shawls to France two hundred years ago. In later ages the Kashmiri Muslim settlers in Punjab and elsewhere were to distinguish themselves as outstanding poets, scholars, and writers.)

Other waves of migrants to the planes consisted of learned pundits. One of them was given lands by Emperor Farrukh Siyar, near a river (*nehr* in Arabic) and therefore they came to be called Nehrus. Successive generations of Kashmiri-pundit settlers of the plains produced a galaxy of Urdu poets, scholars, lawyers and statesmen.

The poorest of the poor were driven out of the Valley due to the proverbial poverty of Kashmir. Being a handsome and gifted people, some of them had become performing artistes. The famous Begum Samroo of the 18th century (who raised her own army), turned a Roman Catholic and married a German military adventurer called General Sombres) was also of Kashmiri descent and began her chequered career as a dancer.

A correspondent writing to the *Calcutta Gazette* on 9 June 1808, says: "Happening to attend a Cashmerian nautch a few nights ago I was struck with the melody and effect of one of the native airs. The song was in the Cashmeree language..."[1]

Hafiz, sung profusely by Khanum Jan and her friends, remained popular for a long time. John Beames in his *Memoirs of a Bengal Civilian* mentions the Persian poet's ghazals being sung by the dancing girls of Bengal around the 1870's.

---

1. *The Good Old Days of Honourable John Company*, Vol. I, by W.H. Carey. Riddhi-India, Calcutta 1980.

The social and economic devastation and collapse of the Old Order forms the backdrop of Hasan Shah's novel. The story illustrates the situation graphically. After the end of the Rohilla Court at Bareilly, Hasan Shah's grandfather who is an eminent physician, comes to the victorious English army's garrison-town, Cawnpore, seeking employment as a tutor. The author himself becomes a petty clerk.

I have been strictly faithful to the text and have not anywhere modernised either the narrative or the dialogue. It is amazing that Hasan Shah wrote the dialogue in the modern form and not as drama, which was to become the style of 19th-century Urdu fiction and which remained with us till the time of Prem Chand. I have only cut down the ornate passages and have also omitted most of the ghazals of Hafiz quoted in the narrative (even the Urdu translator confesses in a footnote that he cut out five pages full of ghazals which described the emotions of the author when he first met Khanum Jan!)

I have also shortened the lengthy love letters exchanged between the hero and the heroine.

Hasan Shah was about twenty when he wrote *Nashtar*. He had no models of novel-writing before him except the lengthy and florid cycles of medieval romances, epics, and allegories. So he does revert from time to time, especially when he is beginning a new chapter, to conventional forms, but after a few lines he comes back to his spontaneous and naturalistic prose. His inclusion of ghazals and Hindi songs is a kind of reportage of the concerts in which Khanum Jan sang and danced. The abundance of poetry also indicates that Indo-Mughal society was basically poetry-oriented and that the English had readily succumbed to its charm and elegance. They could also appreciate the intellectual and mystical content of Persian and Urdu poetry.

The eighteenth century saw the rise of English novel. Apparently Hasan Shah did not know any English (otherwise with his penchant for detail he would have mentioned it.) And obviously the military officers had no time to discuss Richardson, Fielding and Stern with the youthful clerk. Anyway, he would have felt greater affinity with Jane Austen who was five years younger than him and was to write *Pride and Prejudice* in 1796-97.

So here we have a young man who writes an autobiographical piece as a homage to his late wife, without realising that he has become a pioneer of modern Indian novel.

Qurratulain Hyder

In the Name of God, Most Beneficent, Most Merciful

After praising Allah and the Lord Prophet, I record here the story of my early youth when I had found mental and emotional affinity with a person who had simply enthralled and captivated me. For she was an enchantress, an idol who enticed men of piety, and I was intoxicated and stupefied by my frenzied love for her. As the Persian poet Naziri says:

> *No fable is sweeter than mine.*
> *I have chronicled the entire history of Time*
> *Through the story of my own life!*

I hope that if the readers enjoy this true account, they would pray for this sinner, Syed Mohammed Hasan Shah (may God forgive him), that the end of his life may be blissful and that he may be granted merciful pardon in the Hereafter. I also request the readers to draw a curtain over my forgetfulness, mistakes and shortcomings.

Please do pray for me for I am but an errant mortal!

1

My illustrious ancestor Syed Abdullah was a direct descendant of the Lord Prophet. He had migrated first to Yemen, then to Turkestan in Central Asia. One of his descendants called Syed Amir Kalal, achieved great renown as a saint. He had foretold the political ascendancy of the House of Timur. Amir Timur bestowed a jagir upon Amir Kalal's grandson, Amir Shah, who had come to live in Badakhshan.

Amir Shah's grandson, Syed Mirak Shah, also became a famous sufi. He migrated to India and arrived in Lahore during the time of the later Mughals. A lot of people flocked to him and asked him to stay back in Punjab instead of proceeding to Shahjehanabad (Delhi). The mystic, therefore, despatched his follower, Gada Shah, to the Mughal capital to seek an audience with Emperor Farrukh Siyar, (grandson of Aurangzeb). On account of the intrigues of "the kingmakers", the Syed Brothers of Barha, Gada Shah could not see the monarch. Afterwards Farrukh Siyar apologised to the saint, Mirak Shah, and requested him to come over to Delhi. The saint refused. However, thereby hangs another tale.

Meanwhile, Mirak Shah married the daughter of a sufi, called Syed Haqqani, who was a resident of Bandagi, Chakla Kora, Jehanabad. Mirak Shah went to Delhi only once, and that too, during the reign of Emperor Mohammad Shah. He spent most of his life in the vicinity of Lahore and in Sirhind (Haryana).

Syed Mirak Shah had four sons: Syed Mohammad Shah, Ashraf Shah, Arab Shah (my father) and Sher Shah (who became a high-ranking government officer). After the invasions of Nadir Shah (1737) and Ahmad Shah Abdali, my uncle Sher Shah joined the Sircar of the Rohilla Chief, Nawab Najib Khan. Later, my uncle went to live from time to time in Najibabad, Nagina and Dhampur (in district Bijnor). Because of the havoc caused by the Sikhs, my uncle and his brothers shifted to Anwla, Bareilly. Arab Shah got married there. Myself and my younger brothers were born in Bareilly.

After the untimely death of my father, we were brought up by our maternal grandfather, Hakim Mir Mohammad Nawaz. The venerable old man is a renowned doctor and scholar. (His father had come from Balkh. He had joined the Mughal Court and married in Shahjehanabad.)

When my father Arab Shah got married to Mir Mohammad Nawaz's daughter, the famous Hakim was physician to Nawab Enayatullah Khan, son of the Rohilla Chief Hafiz Rehmat Khan (who had died fighting the British in 1774).

After the defeat and collapse of the Government of Hindustan, my grandfather had to become a Munshi to Ming Saheb, Member Council, Camp, Cawnpore.

Ming Saheb was a nephew of the celebrated General Coote. He often travelled to Calcutta on official business. Once when he returned to Cawnpore from Bengal, he became friendly with the fun-loving Col. Helmeddy, Commanding Officer, Cawnpore Cantonment. Consequently he gave up his studies (of Persian and Urdu) for which he had engaged my grandfather. Ming also began to neglect his commercial activities. Once a tidy sum disappeared from his cash box. He mentioned the theft to Grandpa and said that he found no time to look after his private enterprises, and a lot of money was being lost. "Why don't you become my manager, since you have nothing else to do in my household?" he asked his tutor.

Grandpa declined the offer and suggested my name. So Ming Saheb called me and insisted that I join his staff. I accepted on some conditions. No salary was fixed. Ming was a generous, noble and kindly Englishman. He treated me with respect and courtesy,[1] and also gave me valuable presents. His pay was not much, but he had inherited a lot of wealth from his father and his own flourishing business yielded him much profit. He belonged to the breed of large-hearted, bold, and adventurous Englishmen. He made me sole incharge of his business and trusted me implicity. Consequently, some people became jealous and tried to turn him against me. He did not take any notice of their intrigues. I asked him to make his own inquiries into the allegations. Instead of taking any action against me, he gave me the run of the house. Now, I could even engage and dismiss his domestic servants at will.

Ming's current mistress was a woman he had picked up when he was stationed in Farrukhabad. One day she said to him, "Your clerk has been pilfering your goods, Saheb. If you like, I can get my brother to work for you as manager. It would save you further loss."

He strode out of the Bibikhana and came directly to my office. "My bibi says that you are squandering my money, young man", he growled.

---

1. **Translator's Note:** "This was an Englishman of those times. Today they call us native, black man, barbarian. They misbehave with us and crush our rights as much as they can, although we have become much more educated now. Our way of living and abilities have also improved greatly. But a century ago the English who came here were gentlemen, and we were also a decent people. Now both they and us have come equally bad."

"Maybe she is right, Sir," I replied. "I am your well-wisher. Save your business interests in any way you like." I placed the keys on the table, and added, "I cannot stay in your service and go on being victimised by my enemies."

Ming remained silent for some moments and said, "Keep the keys, I will take them from you later."

I was happy that I would leave the job and get rid of the petty rivalries, but the very next day Saheb turned the woman out.

I spoke to him on her behalf and asked him to take her back. He refused.

I said, "In that case, Sir, I, too, must tender my resignation."

He was surprised, "Why do you plead for her? She hates your guts."

"I don't mind her really because nobody can hurt me, if you are on my side."

The Saheb took her back. After a few days he discovered that she was having an affair with the butler. Ming sacked her for good.

At that time I was a greenhorn. My grandfather had brought his family from Bareilly and had settled in a lovely river-side place called Jajmau, a few miles to the east of Cawnpore. Myself, my brother, Hussain Shah, and my cousin, Mir Yusuf Shah—all three of us lived in the military cantonment. The Saheb's house was under construction. He had got a pleasant cottage built for me, too, and had asked me to supervise its decoration. Therefore, for the time being, I had gone to stay with Mir Roshan Ali, who was a friend of my grandfather. I came to Ming's place twice a day to work.

The paymaster of the English army was a thoroughly rakish fellow called Kallan Saheb[1]. He had engaged two companies, male and female, of Kashmiri entertainers, who sang and danced for him in the evenings.

I rode past Collins' bungalow every morning on my way to office. One day as I entered the avenue which led to Ming's house, I was greeted by Mohammad Azam, manager of the nautch-girls' troupe, and an acquaintance of my grandpa. He was standing on a mound. On seeing me, he came down the slope hurriedly and grinned. "How is your esteemed grandfather, Sir?" he enquired politely. "If you do not mind, Sir, do come up to our humble abode."

As a matter of common courtesy I could not refuse, and dismounted. Azam led me up to a canopy, under which a number of singers sat about on cots. They conversed in the Kashmiri language as they obviously asked Azam about me. He told them and they made the customary obeisences.

Azam turned to me. After a little chit-chat he said, "The other day, I heard someone sing lovely ghazals at a concert. I took them down, but I am not too sure if some of the couplets were correct. Would you please check?"

Ceremoniously he gave me a piece of paper.

About a hundred yards from the canvas structure there stood a large tent with an awning in front. Close by, there was a canvas pavilion, and a shack which probably served as their kitchen.

While going through the ghazal I happened to glance at a buxom girl. She had come out of the big tent and was approaching the canopy.

She was dressed in a heavy costume, and wore much jewellery. Her looks dazed me.

---

1. Perhaps Col. Collins whose tomb is situated in Golaganj, Lucknow, and is called Kallan-ki-Lat. (Also see the Afterword).

Now I divided my attention between the ghazal and the camp in front. I was busy reading the verses when a footfall was heard. I looked up and saw that vision again.

She had materialised right there! About twenty or twenty-one, she had wrapped herself in a colourful shawl, and she addressed the men as Ustadji (which is the way singing-women address their music teachers). Azam squatted near me. His son stood beside the divan. She crossed over to stand there. Her rose-pink complexion and exquisite features compelled me to look at her again. After a little while she asked Azam something in her Kashmiri language.

I guessed that she was enquiring about me. Presently, she walked back to her tent.

I was getting late to go to my office, but continued to correct the Persian couplets, hoping to see her again.

Two more trollopes loitered in. One of them was about fourteen years old, fair and plain, also expensively dressed. She had on a white shawl. The other one was in her mid-twenties, plump and dusky. Her clothes were ordinary. They also addressed Azam as Ustadji, and asked about me. "And pray, what are these papers?" One of them added coyly.

"Ghazals. The honourable Syed[1] is very kindly correcting them for me."

They sat down upon a cot. After a while one of them got up and went out. I wished for the first one to reappear so that I could feast my eyes on her.

Tell Moses not to frequent the Mount of Toor.
It's not good to face the Flash again and again.

The woman who had just left, came back, accompanied by another ravishing beauty who could not have been more than seventeen. She had a magnolia face and narcissus

---

1. A descendant of the Prophet.

eyes. She must have ruined the piety of a thousand men. Dressed in fineries, she ambled in, and struck a pose which was utterly devastating. Our eyes met and I was struck by the arrow of love. I became still like a picture and was petrified like a statue. Then I felt a surge of blood in my veins and my heart fluttered helplessly. I felt dizzy and the ghazals' paper slipped from my hand.

With great difficulty I took hold of myself and wondered if so much beauty was possible to exist. It was incredible. Perhaps God had created her with His own hands. The catastrophe I had been pre-destined to face was right there in front of me!

The first woman came back and all three sat together on the *charpoy*. The dazzling nymph threw a mischievous glance at me.

One of the women asked her mentor, "Ustadji, has any couplet been corrected yet by his honour?"

"Yes, several," he said.

"Is this gentleman a poet?" she asked.

"No," I replied.

Mohammad Azam turned to the enchantress and began eulogising me and my grandfather. I bent down my head, still in a state of bewilderment.

The Moon-faced One said, "He is not quite well, is he?"

"Can't help it," I replied.

"What is the matter, Sir?" asked Mohammad Azam.

"Headache, due to lack of sleep," I answered shortly. "I am sitting here only because of you."

"You do look distraught, Sir. The paper also slipped from your fingers. Never mind. You can make the corrections some other time."

The first woman spoke, "Ustadji, how long have you known young Munshiji?"

"I have the privilege of being an acquaintance of his august grandfather."

The woman cut him short and addressed me, "Do come here again."

"I will, if I get some respite from the work I do for my master."

"Everybody has masters! No one is free." The Beauty retorted merrily and walked away.

I was astonished by her sudden departure. Mohammad Azam noticed my state and said, "Sir, you certainly have a nasty headache. You need some rest."

On reaching my bungalow which was still under construction, I threw myself down on a cot. There was no office work to do. As the day wore on, my younger brothers arrived. I continued to pretend that I was unwell, and returned to my host Munshi Roshan Ali's house.

After a sleepless night, the following morning I rode off to office as usual. I cantered on, hoping to meet Mohammad Azam or his son on the way. They could not be seen. I didn't feel like going up to their camp uninvited. They could have insulted me, too.

So in the evening I returned to my lodgings gloomily, like the previous day.

2

My 'illness' had become known. Mr. Ming himself came to see me. I repeated the story about my migraine. After he left, my condition became worse. On the third day again I lingered a while near the tents and then proceeded to my bungalow. In the evening the workmen grew more noisy in their fuss and bustle. And I felt I was going round the bend. I gave the purse to my brothers to pay the men their daily wages. Then I mounted my steed and made for Paymaster Collins' compound. Mohammad Azam's son saw me and ran off to inform his father.

The troupe manager appeared on the slope, salaamed, and called me uphill, saying he had a request to make.

I was too happy to accompany him to their encampment. "My employer has arranged a saint's feast," he said. "Your honour being a Syed, and a descendant of saints yourself, kindly consecrate the food, and bless us with your holy presence."

Azam made me sit in the tent and went out. After a few minutes he returned, along with a pious-looking man who kissed my feet. Azam introduced him, "He is the owner of this Company."

"Please Sir, be so kind as to betake yourself to my tent," the old man said humbly.

When I entered the big tent I felt as though I had come out of the Region of Darkness and hit the Spring of Eternal Life.[1] First my eyes fell upon a fair woman of about thirty. She sat on a *divan* with great dignity, a quilted shawl around her. She seemed to be the joint-owner of the troupe, the way she was queening it over. She rose to her feet, salaamed effusively and offered me a camp-chair.

A Kashmiri faqir was also present, along with an elderly woman who had covered her head with a scarf. She was

---

1 In Islamic legend the inaccessible "Spring of Life" is located somewhere in the Caucasus Mountains. One can reach it only after crossing the Region of Darkness. The waters of this spring grant eternal life to human beings. Only the prophet Khizr could reach it and he became immortal. He is the mystical figure dressed in green (symbolising eternal youth) who is sometimes found walking along lonely waterways. He is the Unseen Guide who helps travellers who have lost their way. The Spring of Life and Khwaja Khizr are favourite metaphors in classical Persian and Urdu literature.

busy making arrangements for the sacred feast. Food was being cooked in huge cauldrons.

When everything was ready, Mohammad Azam asked me to recite the benedictions.

"This venerable dervish," I replied, "should do so."

They insisted that I must. I asked the men and women to stand in separate rows and began the Opening Verse.

And there she was, standing in the women's row!

So help me God. I prolonged the prayers and went on and on till the time arrived for the twilight service. I consecrated the food and went across to the men's tent. There I said my evening prayers. After which I buttonholed Azam and asked, "My good man, who on earth are these people, anyway? What is all this going on over here?"

"The person I had asked to kiss your feet, Sir, he is also called Azamji. He used to be a merchant. Clever fellow, but it happened that he had to suffer heavy losses in his business. The hag with the kerchiefed head belongs to the caste of singing-women. Her name is Chameli Jan. She had become his mistress. After he went bankrupt, she advised him to give up his trading activities. 'I shall collect some women,' she said, 'and proceed to Hindustan. There I shall get up a band of singers and nautch-girls, and tour the land.'

"Since Azamji had become penniless and he is under her thumb, anyway, he agreed. The dame with the quilted wrap is our queen-bee. She is called Mirzai. They took her along from Kashmir. She is also Azamji's mistress, on the quiet.

"They came down to Jammu and got hold of the pretty girl, known as Gulbadan, you saw first that day. She is our main source of income.

"From Jammu they came over to Lahore and recruited some female relatives of Chameli Jan.

"Chameli Jan had a daughter by her first husband. She was known as Saheb Jan. A Pathan chieftain had employed her as his concubine. Later he married her forcibly. A daughter was born. The Sardar died. Saheb Jan was persecuted by her in-laws. She ran away and returned to her mother, Chameli Jan. The poor girl died soon afterwards. Our leader, Azamji, has adopted her orphaned daughter, Khanum Jan. He dotes on her. He has given her an excellent academic education, too."

"Which one is she?" My heart sank.

"The one in rice-field-green shawl. She stood next to Mirzai, at the time of the benediction."

Ah, I said to myself. So her name is Khanum Jan.

"Because of Azamji, Mirzai loves her and treats her as her own daughter. The rest of the troupe also look after her with great affection. Azamji did not like her to dance and sing, but her grandmother Chameli Jan, is a hardheaded Madam. She has got her trained as a dancing-girl. Still, Azamji wants her to marry a gentleman and become a respectable housewife. Some Englishmen proposed to take her into concubinage. She hasn't still entered the oldest profession because Azamji and Mirzai would not like it."

"Who was the young girl with the white shawl?" I asked.

"Bi Jan. She is a niece of Chameli Jan. Hollier Saheb[1] had employed her on a salary of five hundred rupees a month. He went away. She stayed back. Now, only Gulbadan gets three hundred rupees as Kallan Saheb's mistress. He gives fifty rupees to Khanum Jan as pin-money. They have to give a weekly performance for which they are paid thirty rupees per evening. The paymaster also bears their kitchen expenses and has given a lot of jewellery to Gulbadan."

---

1. According to Iqtadar Alam Khan this was perhaps the famous Maj. Polier whose name was misspelled by the calligraphist.

"Why is Khanum Jan decked up like a bride today?" was my next question.

"Her late mother used to celebrate her birthday with great fanfare. Fifty to sixty rupees' worth of food was distributed to the beggars. The saints' feast was arranged. Azamji has continued the tradition.

"The girl has inherited a casketful of jewellery from her mother. Azamji has also given her many ornaments. She is loaded, you may say, the richest girl of this band! As for her intelligence, refinement and good nature, she has no peer!"

I was about to take my leave when a maid came in and announced: "Mirzai says, don't let him go. Please come up to her tent."

"It is getting late," I protested.

Azamji was adamant. I had to give in.

Outside, soup was being ladled out to a throng of destitutes. In the tent Mirzai was waiting for me. She used much florid language, imploring me to stay for dinner. "Trays will be sent down to your bungalow, Sir, but do have a bite with us, here, too. If you had come in the daytime, you would have enjoyed our music as well."

"My fault," Azam put in. "I didn't inform him."

"Usually I do not eat out and I do not like spiceless dishes!"

Mirzai got the hint that by 'spiceless' I meant 'without music'. She answered cheerfully, "We shall provide the spices and the dressing, too, though it would not be the same as our lunchtime session. Still, we will sing for you as best as we can."

She told the maid to call Bi Jan, and asked Azamji to summon Siddique-ji and other instrumentalists.

Presently, Bi Jan, Gulbadan and Umda trooped in. Mirzai said to them, "Mir[1] Saheb is young and carefree. He

---
1. Mir is another term of respect for a Syed.

likes to listen to his fiddlers while he eats. Entertain him well."

The musicians came in and began to tune their instruments.

I said to myself: everybody has turned up except Khanum Jan. That's too bad.

"Perhaps the Birthday Girl has no interest in tuneful activities," I uttered aloud.

"Oh no, Sir! Our Khanum Jan has not had much formal training but she is the finest crooner of us all," said Gulbadan promptly.

"In that case I am surprised that she is not here."

Mirzai was taken aback by my remark. She asked Gulbadan about her adopted daughter.

"We were enjoying the hulla baloo of the lumpen being fed, when Seoti called us in. Khanum Jan said she had a headache and would like to be excused. 'Tell Mother I am not well,' she said."

Gulbadan's information upset me. I thought she had sensed my obsession for her and had started playing games.

"Never mind," said Mirzai. "Now that we know you, Sir, we shall invite you to a proper concert, and Khanum Jan shall warble for you."

"That's all right," I said dryly. "I am not terribly fond of music. Your hospitality induced me to become so informal and ask for a song or two. It's a pity all the same, that a person whose birthday is being celebrated should not be present. Perhaps she does not like me to come here."

"Not at all, Sir," Mirzai protested. "My Khanum is not rude or bad-mannered. She had a late night because of the celebrations, and does have a headache. I will go and fetch her."

"You need not," I replied curtly.

"No. Khanum Jan must come," said Azamji vehemently. Mirzai hurried out.

"Bi Jan!" said Gulbadan silkily. "Mir Saheb is so sweet, isn't he? And he seems to remember such *tomes* of ghazals. Please, Mir Saheb, do recite something for us, too."

Mirzai returned with Khanum Jan.

I recited Sheikh Hazeen's[1] ghazal which aptly expressed the turmoil in my heart.

> *Whose radiance leaves me wonderstruck?*
> *Whose footfall sets my heart afire?*
> *My laments take away all kindness from her heart!*
> *And when she tries to remember me*
> *A certain forgetfulness overtakes her*
> *I am a prey not worth hunting for.*
> *I am so ashamed of my worthlessness before my hunter.*

Khanum Jan avoided looking at me and averted her face.

"What's the matter, child?" Azam asked her. "How are you?"

"Bad head," she mumbled.

The women broke into a song.

Khanum Jan sang a ghazal of Hafiz Shirazi. The love lyric had an obvious effect on me. I could not control my tears.

Chameli Jan's maid came in and said to Mirzai, "Madam wants you to supervise the food trays before they are sent out to friends."

---

1. Sheikh Hazeen was an eminent 18th-century Persian poet who lived and died in Benares, a city he loved dearly.

Mirzai excused herself and said to Mohammed Azam, "Mir Saheb is in love. Just look at him!"

"I am in love with you!" I grinned.

"How lucky of me!" she answered jovially.

"I am not the stuff great lovers are made of." I said soberly. "Love is too big a load for my poor heart and confused mind to carry. The thing is that excellent poetry always has its impact on sensitive souls."

"Yes, indeed," agreed Gulbadan. "Mir Saheb himself is so lovable. Dames must be making a beeline for him. The lucky one would attract his attention."

"Why don't you try and dip your hands in the flowing Ganges? Send him your proposition. You won't get another wealthy patron like him," said Khanum Jan archly.

Gulbadan ignored her catty remark. The maid appeared again. "Bibi is very annoyed, she is tired waiting for you, Mirzai."

I thanked the hosts for their hospitality.

"Our servants do not know your address," said Mirzai. "Send your groom up here to take the food to your house. And do come again."

"I will, if she is a bit courteous," I replied, pointing towards Khanum Jan.

"Gulbadan has fallen flat for you. Both of you can wait for each other's courteous response," she retorted sourly.

"Suits me fine!" I said lightly and bade them goodnight.

I came back to my place, both happy and sad. I had met her again and talked to her. At the same time I regretted the emotional mess I had landed myself in.

I started composing ghazals in Rekhta[1] and wondered how to meet her, and what would be the result of this one-sided foolhardy passion of mine?

I was sick with anxiety. Grandfather came to know of my ill-health and rushed down from Jajmau. He examined me and prescribed the medicine for fever and headache. I laughed quietly.

Meanwhile, my little bungalow had been furnished and was ready for occupation. Mr. Ming came to Roshan Ali's residence to see me. He asked me why I didn't shift to my own house now. I was reluctant because from my present abode I had to pass by Khanum Jan's camp twice a day on my way to the office and back. And that entailed a chance of meeting her. Now that opportunity would be gone.

Fortunately, the day my luggage was being transported from Roshan Ali's place to the cantonment, I saw Mohammad Azam again. He happened to be standing on the same hillock where I had met him the first time. Instead of inviting me to his tent, he gave me bad news. Paymaster Kallan Saheb was sailing for Calcutta and the entertainers' band had lost their job. Now they, too, were planning to decamp.

I was thunderstruck. Khanum Jan could not be seen too, for she did not come out of her tent. I rode on to my new cottage, feeling miserable.

Another restless night. When I fell asleep I dreamed of my father. He said, "Do not fret. Believe in Providence. Occupy yourself with the reading of books." Then my father quoted a Persian ghazal of Lala Ram Narain.[2]

Love is freedom from bondage
Love is to run to and fro on the path of the Quest[3]

---

1. Old name of Urdu.
2. Please see notes.
3. The allusion is to Abraham's wife Hagar who ran on burning sands between the hillocks of Safa and Marwa, looking for water.

*In our search for Truth why do we worry about tomorrow?
My friend, Love is life!*

After which he disappeared.

Feeling a lot better in the morning, I said my prayers, took my medicine and opened the carved chest of books. The very first volume I lay my hands on turned out to be my father's tattered diary. I carried it gingerly to my bed and began turning its pages. Then I noticed a number of mystical charts, occult prayers and talismans. One of the special prayers could prevent Azamji's departure for Chunargarh. I discovered that today was the very day of the week marked for the particular recitation. I took it to be a good omen and intoned the mystical formula.

In the afternoon I visited the singers' camp. Nobody was there. I sent my syce to Kallan Saheb's compound on the pretext of finding out about the Paymaster's voyage to Calcutta.

After that I rode out to the river-front.

When I came back, the servant was already there. He told me that in the compound he had met Mohammad Azam who told him that Kallan Saheb had gone to Calcutta a couple of days ago, and that he had paid off the company for good.

"We are also leaving," the troupe manager had informed my servant. "We will set up camp along the river bank and wait there for a good boat. None has stopped by so far. In the meantime many Englishmen have sent us their offers. They would like to employ us but not one of them seems so generous as to maintain the entire company. So we have decided to go downriver to Fort Chunar and join Hollier Saheb over there. We had promised him that we would turn up whenever we were free."

The information aggravated my anxiety no end. After a few days I sent the syce again to Mohammad Azam. He came running to see me. He looked distracted.

"Whatever happened now?" I asked.

"Gulbadan the... the bitch... she ran away with an Englishman last night. Can't be traced anywhere. She was our sole breadwinner. She ran the show. What do we do now? Where can we go? We will have to starve..."

"God is the great Provider. Don't worry. Still, what are your plans?"

"We have decided to stay back for the time being, here in Cawnpore. Chameli Jan will take a fast boat to the east. We are told that the Englishman and Gulbadan have gone in that direction.

"What on earth shall we do? Old Azamji will not allow Khanum Jan to join this lucrative profession. Bi Jan is not much in demand, being so plain, and nobody would pay her much, anyway. Please, Mir Saheb, give me a charm or a talisman to help us in this crisis."

"Occult prayers help if they are recited within twenty-four hours of a calamity. Now they would not be effective. If you had informed me immediately after Gulbadan's disappearance, I would have certainly given you some amulet."

Still, to comfort, him I intoned a special prayer for the recovery of lost persons, and clapped thrice in the prescribed manner. Then I scribbled out a charm for him. He took it gratefully and left.

3

A ruffian called Mithoo the Pimp used to work as a procurer for Ming Saheb. I sent for him and gave him some *bakhshish*. Then I asked him if he knew Azamji's outfit. He said he knew it very well indeed.

Four Kashmiri troupes were staying in Cawnpore at that time. Mithoo, of course, knew all of them. He was also aware of Gulbadan's elopement and Azamji and company's intending departure for Fort Chunar.

I asked him to recommend this lot to Ming for employment.

He went straight to the big bungalow and began praising the itinerant performers. Soon he convinced Ming of their excellence.

"But they are too expensive. I can't afford such luxury," said Ming.

"Gulbadan, their prima donna, was coveted by warlords and chieftains. She just upped and ran away. Since they have nobody as lascivious and attractive to replace her, their sights have lowered. Besides, Saheb, among all the Europeans posted out here, you are known to be the most fun-loving. If you engage a famous company like this one, it will only enhance your reputation..."

After his siesta Ming summoned me, and said, "When I threw that Farrukhabadi woman out, I had decided never to keep an Indian mistress. But today Mithoo has made this rather interesting suggestion. What is your opinion, sagagious Munshi?"

"You know best, Saheb, but it would be an expensive affair. Sheer waste of money."

"You are right."

"Personally, I shall never advise you, but when you take a fancy to something or someone, you never think twice."

"You are right."

"If I were you I would not..."

"I have seen their performance twice in Collin's

drawing room. The women sing beautifully. They are fine dancers, too."

"You have already made up your mind. Why ask me?"

He laughed. "Don't be cross. I will do what you say."

"Still, first let's hear them tomorrow. I will employ the band only after you approve of them!"

"As your well-wisher I would not approve of them. Since you are adamant, go ahead. But do keep in mind that they would cost you a fortune. And if you dismiss them after a while it would bring you discredit."

"Why do you go on harping on expenses? I am not stingy." He said angrily and called Mithoo again. He told the tout that he was first going to hear the male vocalists.

Afterwards the procurer hastened to my office. I told him that I had my own reasons to advise Ming Saheb against the proposal.

The following morning Mohammad Azam's son Afzal arrived at my house. Respectfully he conveyed to me his father's and Mirzai's salaams and said, "Beg to state, Sir, that today we are going to present our *mujra* before the Saheb Bahadur. Please put in a word on our behalf. You have enormous influence over him and he was great regard for you."

"Don't worry. I will do my best."

"Mithoo says, 'You all can't get the employment without Munshi's recommendation.' Please help us. We are in dire straits. We will always be grateful to you."

I assured him again of my help and thanked God that he had so unexpectedly made these people dependent on me for their livelihood.

After Ming Saheb had had his *hazri*, they arrived with their orchestra. Since it was a kind of audition, they put in all their expertise and talent in the performance. They sang their ghazals so soulfully that Ming began to shake his head and stamp his feet in ecstatic frenzy.

Since I was madly in love, I too was deeply moved by the lyrics. I even shed many tears.

They sang for a couple of hours.

Afterwards, Ming took me inside and said, "Splendid, aren't they?"

"If I knew they were so good I would not have let them come here."

"Why?"

"You have liked them so much now you will engage them. And then you may dismiss the bunch."

"Why?"

"They are a frightfully expensive proposition."

"Don't you go on repeating that," he flared up again.

I took Mithoo aside and told him to inform Azam that I had recommended them strongly. "You can go now. Bring the female band tonight."

Ming asked me if I had given the chap any *bakshish*. "They shall get it tonight, with knobs on," I replied.

He laughed, and said in Persian, "You do not feel like spending money on the bibies! What kind of young man are you?"

He invited his English friends for dinner that evening. The dance performance began at eight o' clock. Saheb sent a *harkara* over to me.

I said I was busy with my office work. The *harkara* went back to the big bungalow and rushed back with the message,

"Leave your bloody work and come."

Ming made me sit next to him. In accordance with the convention of *mujras*, Khanum Jan began the song of felicitation.

She knew many ghazals of Hafiz and rendered them well. Ming kept asking me their meaning and relayed my explanations to his English friends. They were all spellbound and they, too, waved their hands and stamped their feet, like the possessed.[1]

Mr. John Head and Mr. Warren gave two gold *mohurs* each to Mirzai.

The programme went on till midnight.

Ming turned towards me, "It is twelve o'clock, Munshi."

"You hand them the *pandaan* and the *chowghara* yourself, to indicate that the party is over."

He did so. The entertainers took their leave in a courtly manner.

In the morning when Ming saw me in the office he said, "Well, Hasan Shah, you have fallen in love, haven't you!"

"Yes Sir?"

"The way you howled when that trollope sang..."

"Good music has its effect on animals, too. I am a human being!" I grinned. "I had been equally moved when the men sang in the morning."

"I will order Mithoo to bring them over, bag and baggage. Suggest some place for them to stay. All of them can't be accommodated in the *bibikhana*."

"They can pitch their tents right here."

"Where?"

"In front of your house, Sir."

---

1. "Monkeys' gestures" — The Urdu translator Sajjad Hussain's comment.

"There is not much space in my compound. Look, you have plenty of land in between the pigeon house and the female quarters near your cottage. It's quite secluded too."

"The land is uneven. Lots of ups and downs, Sir. The ground in front of your place is level."

"Yes, but it faces the public thoroughfare and my colonel passes by on this road. This won't do. You had better get your own land cleared."

"As you wish. If you like I can even vacate my house for them."

Ming lost his temper.

"You really don't want them to come here, do you?"

Seeing his anger I went out at once and called the *beldars* to level my plot of land.

Mithoo arrived with the news that *they* had arrived.

Saheb came out of his verandah, laughing, and welcomed them heartily.

I supervised the workmen some more and came home, quite perturbed. Gulbadan had vanished, otherwise Ming would have taken her as his new bibi. Now only Khanum Jan was there. How with my sense of honour, I would tolerate the outrage. I wished I had never met these people or recommended them to my British employer. I could have kicked myself for creating the dreadful situation myself.

4

The members of the troupe were busy discussing their future. Their survival, they said, depended on Khanum Jan. If she did not become an "employee" of Ming Saheb, they would starve. They persuaded old Azamji, her foster -

father, to accept the proposal. Mithoo was the middleman.

Her renumeration was fixed at rupees two hundred and fifty a month, plus thirty rupees per *mujra*. When the news was brought to me, I was shocked out of my wits and didn't know what to do.

Presently a *harkara* turned up with the message that the Saheb wished to see me.

Ming was standing on the freshly prepared camp site. He was surrounded by the men and women of the nautch company. He noticed my flushed face and whispered to Khanum Jan:

"Look, my munshi is sulking. He does not want you people to live here!"

"I don't care if he is so grumpy," she replied curtly.

"Don't say that. I am quite scared of him. Why, he may even beat up both of us!"

"Speak for yourself. He dare not show his temper to me."

I overhead their conversation.

Mirzai came forward and greeted me. Ming repeated his words about me.

"That's all right," she replied smoothly. "He is a noble Syed. If he chastises us for something, it would be our great good fortune. We are so low, we are inferior to even his handmaids."

"You say this, and Khanum Jan says she couldn't care less!" Ming remarked.

"Khanum is a foolish girl, Sir. She is just being silly."

Ming laughed and said, "I hereby hand over Khanum Jan to our grumpy Hasan Shah." He turned round to me.

"Now Hasan Shah, go ahead and admonish her. You become her teacher. I have given her to you."

Good omen! But I said, "Saheb, ever since you have met these women you are so happy that you have started pulling my leg. You or Mohammad Azam can be their mentor. They are no concern of mine."

I turned to go home.

"Where are you off to? I had called you here to discuss the problem of the tents!"

"Right now you are in a mood to crack jokes. You had better go home. I will do the needful."

"Well, I will go." He added softly to Khanum Jan, "See how temperamental he is!"

"You must have taken a fancy to him, Saheb," she remarked sourly. "Otherwise you wouldn't pamper him so!"

"He looks after my business deals most efficiently. I can't afford to lose him. Why, if I show him the slightest indifference, he would just resign and go away, he is so inordinately sensitive!"

They were talking in undertones. Nevertheless, I could hear them and feigned ignorance of what they were saying about me. Then I busied myself with the job in hand and walked away.

I got their camp pitched and returned home. I was extremely agitated about the predicament faced by Khanum Jan. In the evening I took out my father's notebook again and recited a prayer for the safety of the poor girl's honour and chastity.

As a matter of fact, Khanum Jan was very upset too, and I didn't know how to save her from the impending disaster. As night fell, the harlots dressed her up in her fineries and sent her across to Ming's house.

When the Saheb made amorous advances she simply went haywire and raised the roof. The Briton was taken by surprise. He called Mirzai and shouted, "When this bibi had not agreed, why did you force her to come to me?"

Mirzai fell at the girl's feet and beseeched her not to be so pig-headed. Khanum Jan refused. The Saheb said, "Take her away, lest she kills herself. I do not need to take women forcibly. Just send Bi Jan over here. But I won't pay her more than a hundred rupees a month."

Mirzai must have thought that in that situation even hundred rupees were good enough.

She sent Bi Jan to Ming's bungalow. Khanum Jan's virtue was saved.

The night passed. In the morning the gang made a lot of noise in their tent as they screamed and argued back and forth and gave hell to poor Khanum Jan. She continued to weep incessantly.

She cried so much that her eyelids became puffy. Ming heard about her plight and came over. "Why is she crying now?" he asked, surprised.

"She is not crying," said Mirza bitterly. "She is ruining our prospects. The wretch may live or die for all we care. She may drown in her tears if she likes. We are busy lamenting our own fate. How would we manage to exist on a measly hundred rupees, I ask you."

Now dear Readers, see how God works His miracles:

Ming said: "If Khanum Jan stops weeping, I will fix a salary for her, too."

As soon as Khanum Jan heard these words she wiped her tears and went over to sit near the Englishman. "I was crying for two reasons," she began sweetly. "One: I don't want to start this kind of life for only a short while more, because I know that I live in a bawdy house and cannot eventually escape my fate. Second: I cried when I thought of their hardships. How would they survive on a hundred rupees a month? And I am the sole cause of their distress."

"Fair enough," said Ming. "I will give you fifty a month to buy yourself some fruit."[1]

"How can I accept only fifty when Bi Jan gets a hundred?"

"Bi Jan agreed to sleep with me. If you had been so inclined, I was going to pay you two hundred and fifty a month, anyway."

"So why do you want to pay me fifty now?"

"So that you don't weep and be so unhappy. Besides, Bi Jan is a bore. You are an interesting person to talk to."

"So why are you giving me only fifty?" she asked slyly. "People who attach greater value to good nature and good conversation prefer those qualities to other things."

Ming burst out laughing. "Bi Jan being your own peer, you don't want her to become your superior! Alright, I will give you a hundred rupees, too. But don't you howl again."

"I shan't. Why would I if I have noble admirers like you!" she said coquettishly.

After Ming left, Khanum Jan arranged for another Thanksgiving feast. She was grateful to Providence not only because her honour had remained intact but because she had been assured of an increment. Otherwise her people would have driven her crazy with their barbed comments.

In the afternoon Saheb told me about the new arrangement.

"Why pay Khanum Jan for nothing?" I asked.

"She was crying her eyes out. I didn't like to see her sob so bitterly."

I came home and I too thanked God for His mercy.

---

1. Mewakhori, an Iranian term for pin-money.

5

Now that I felt relieved, I began to decorate my small bungalow cheerfully. One of my verandahs faced the singers' camp. I had it furnished as my lounge.

I spent most of my time here and could catch a glimpse or two of Khanum as she went about in her enclosure.

Sometimes I saw her at the Saheb's musical soirees, but found no occasion to visit the colourful tents.

A month passed and I could not get in touch with her, although whenever she came to chat with Ming and I was also there, she always started some topic on which I would have an argument with my employer. That was her way of teasing me.

One day she asked Ming's permission to go to his garden. He took her there himself. The bower was aglow with tulips, chrysanthemums and jasmines. She quoted a relevant Hafiz couplet:

My rivals in the garden, like the tulip and the rose,
Pick up a wine-cup each, remembering their beloved's face.

"How do you interpret this?" she asked Ming. He told her, according to his limited understanding of Persian poetry.

"No," she said flatly.

"Call the Munshi," Ming commanded Ram Kishan, the gardener.

When I got there I found them all enjoying themselves among the roses. Ming asked Khanum to recite the couplet again. Both of them gave their own interpretations.

I gave mine.

"Hafiz says that every rival has taken up a goblet in the memory of his beloved."

"You say that everyone has sipped some wine remembering his beloved. Our Khanum Jan says that every one liked the wine glass which resembled the complexion of his beloved. Which one could be the correct meaning?" Ming asked.

The discussion went on. Khanum as usual had the upper hand! Ming gave me a few marigolds.

Ram Kishan brought us a load of bouquets.

On the way back I ran into Mirzai who was hurrying down to the park. "We were better off in our old camp," she said briskly. "At least you visited us there twice. Now you have become so indifferent!"

"Too much office work, you know." After a pause I added, "Look, you are employed by my master. It would not be proper to start socialising with you. It may lead to complications."

"Why? I will take his permission right now."

"Oh, no. Don't do that. You will make it more awkward. I will come sometime."

I returned home, wondering why Khanum Jan always liked to belittle and annoy me in front of Ming. Why was she trying to harm me?

Suddenly I heard Ming's voice. He had walked across to my own front-garden. "We are here to look at your flowers. Come out!" he shouted.

I found Khanum Jan, Bi Jan and Mirzai strolling down the garden path.

I opened the gate. My servants started the fountains.

"Saheb, what a wonderful taste your Munshi has!— What an enchanting garden he has laid out," exclaimed Mirzai. "But alas, he does not care for us, never comes to our place!"

"He is a bashful and finicky young man. Hardly goes anywhere. He does not bother about my English friends. He cares little for me. He is like that."

"Your snooty Munshi may like it or not, I am going to pluck some of his flowers," announced Khanum Jan and went into action, till Mirzai cried, "Hey, don't rob his garden, wench!"

Khanum wore the blossoms in her pierced ears, gave a marigold to Ming and crushed a tulip with her fingers before she passed it to me.

They spent the entire evening in my garden.

I had another restless night. After saying my early morning prayer I got into my *boocha* and went out to the river.

After coming back I told the bearers to keep the litter in the verandah for my outing in the evening. In the afternoon I got into the wheelless brougham, closed its windows and began to brood.

Suddenly something was thrown out from the side of the camp. It hit the window of the *boocha* and fell down. I picked it up. It was a ruby-studded gold ring. I looked across at the main tent. Somebody had made a little chink in the canvas and was peeping out.

I quoted some Hafiz aloud. She flung back another couplet which said: *"The destination is full of danger and the aim is not manifest. Still, no difficulty in the world is such that cannot be surmounted!"*

The following morning as I stepped out, an urchin came running and said that he was the son of Azamji's cook and that his name was Rahmullah.

"And what brings you here, sonny?" I asked.

"Nothing. I was loitering around and spotted you. I have often seen you sitting here, lonely and forlorn. Can I be of any help?"

"You are a child. What can you do?"

"Children can be useful!"

"I am in love with one of those damsels."

"I had thought as much!"

"Sit down. Listen. Her name is Khanum Jan."

The boy seemed to have been well-trained. He pointed towards the tent. "Why her? She is arrogant, thinks no end of herself. I am her foster-brother. My mother used to be her wet-nurse. Still, why should I tell lies? She is conceited. Compared to her Bi Jan is a paragon of virtues. Good-tempered and gentle. And she likes you a lot. In fact, one day she said, Munshiji is such a fine person and ever so handsome. Whereupon Khanum Jan retorted, 'I don't think he is all that wonderful.' Therefore, Munshiji," continued the boy, "you ought to fall in love with Bi Jan!"

"Love is something spontaneous and irrational. Even if your foster-sister does not care for me, I can't help adoring her." I told him to recite a particular couplet of Hafiz to her on my behalf.

"Why don't you write it down on a piece of paper? I will give it to her," he suggested.

I gave him two rupees which he did not accept.

I looked in front, and found her peering through the slit. Obviously she had despatched the lad. In the afternoon he came back with the query: "She asks, have you been in love before?"

"No."

"She would like to know: what is it that you want really?"

Thus we began exchanging our highly literary and poetic messages and letters.

One day Rahmullah asked me, "Sir, are you married?"

"No. Why do you ask?"

I read her letter again at night and realised that she had spelt out all the troubles and dangers our secret love affair entailed.

I wrote back that for her sake I was willing to face all consequences.

The same day it happened that Khanum Jan told Mirzai to arrange for the Feast of All-Night Cooking.

The custom among these folk was that once during winter-time, each family, by turn, had a music and dance session at home, while the *shab-deg* (night cauldron) full of meat, chicken, partridges and turnips was cooked in gravy. It simmered till daybreak.

In the morning the guests had it as their breakfast before they left.

The following day I saw guests arriving at the main tent. Rahmullah gave me the report:

It transpired that an affluent and classy demi-monde by the name of Mewa Jan lived in the city of Cawnpore. She had, in her employment, a genteel Syed widow who taught Mewa's daughter how to read the Holy Quran. On her deathbed the resident teacher entrusted her own little girl to Mewa Jan for she had no relatives who could take care of the child.

The courtesan had brought up the orphan with affection and had decided to marry her to a gentleman. She was going to give her considerable dowry as well and was about to go to Lucknow to find a suitable Syed husband for her.

Now, Mewa Jan and her ward also came to the All-Night Cooking Feast. Since that girl lived in purdah, the hosts, led by Khanum Jan, had made special arrangements for her seclusion.

At sundown Rahmullah brought me Khanum Jan's letter, and said, "Before you read it, just stand aside at the back of the tent."

I ventured out. The boy lifted the curtain and I saw Khanum Jan and another attractive girl walking about hand-in-hand inside the enclosure. I could see her at leisure. The moment the girl's eyes met mine Khanum Jan rushed forward and dropped the curtain.

"Now you can read the letter," Rahmullah said.

"So, you say you are prepared to face all troubles for the sake of your love. Kindly tell me: Have my looks and youth attracted you? In that case imagine me as an old hag, for beauty vanishes in no time. Are you fascinated by my singing voice?

"That, too, will go with age. I will sound like a broken pitcher.

"I am not frightfully rich and fortunately you don't care for wealth. So, please, tell me what on earth is it for which you have fallen head over heels...? If my assets, looks and voice have maddened you, then it is not love. It is mere lust, it would vanish as quickly as it has appeared. And it is not reliable. You belong to a sacred lineage. Your elders and relatives would never like this match and would compel you to marry in your own society. Therefore, do not delay your marriage. You may even consider this girl I have just shown you. She is high-born like you and shall get ample dowry. Her relatives would feel honoured to marry her to you. The match can be arranged easily. In case you have already been betrothed, please complete the rites. Nothing would be more sensible than that. Otherwise, remember: to remain enmeshed in this love business would be utter insanity on your part and would become a lifelong problem for you."

What an intelligent woman and how heartless! How do I deal with her logic and how do I trap this wild deer...? I read the letter again and again at night and wrote back:

"O star of the Zodiac of Loveliness. Your *toomar*[1] of good advice reached me and I marvel at your foresight and common sense. To be precise, here are the points why I adore you: God has bestowed you with the following qualities:

"Sense of honour, and self-respect, also modesty to a proper degree.

"Chastity.

"Politeness, sweet speech, brilliance.

"Steadfastness.

"The ability to understand human nature, good judgement, loyalty are qualities I have not yet tested in you but a person with all these characteristics must be extraordinary. It is a pity that you are trapped amongst a kind of people who have nothing to do with these qualities.

"The pretty girl you kindly showed me cannot be compared to you. And thanks for your pearls of wisdom regarding my marriage."

She wrote back to say that she was orphaned in infancy and was brought up by Azamji and Mirzai, that they always swore that they would not allow her to become a whore.

"Knowing them as I did, I never believed in their promises. These people do not have the fear of God in their hearts. And even if I believed in their words, I always wondered what kind of husband they would find for me. He could be lecherous, or illiterate or crude. But then you did see how they went back on their promises and tried

---

1. Many yards long document which was rolled up in bundles.

their worst to sell me into concubinage. It was only by the grace of God that I was saved. But how much disgrace I have had to face! The shock is melting my bones. If it was not sinful to commit suicide, I would have killed myself.

"The first day when Azamji praised you when I saw you I prayed to God that they marry me to you. When the suggestion came to join Mr. Ming's entourage, I thought you had become interested in me, and it must have been your suggestion.

"My guess was correct. From that day I assumed an attitude of hostility towards you in the presence of Ming and others, so that nobody would guess my true feelings for you.

"I quote a Hindi *tappa:* You would find many of my kind. I will get none like you even though I roam the earth.

"I have decided to spend the rest of my life with you. Keep my sercrets I have told you. I refused your offer of marriage just to test you. But I repeat and swear on your head that if your folk want you to marry elsewhere too, do not say 'no' because of me. It is stupid and meaningless to try to bind men to such promises. Because it is almost impossible for a man to remain monogamous all his life. However, I will tell you about some other promises which are imperative for people in love and which both you and I will have to keep. But do not become conceited..."

6

Now it became our wont that just before sunset she would come out and stand behind the screen of thick red cloth which surrounded her tent. I sat down in my verandah, and both of us had a delightful exchange of quotations from famous ghazals...

One evening Ming invited his English friends to dinner. It was followed by the usual song-and-dance routine. According to custom, the guests sat in the place of honour. The rest of the audience was assembled on the other end of the reception hall.

To the right of Mr. Ming and myself there stood the band of musicians. That particular evening, the place was so overcrowded that the host had to sit right at the end of the row, and I was squeezed between the wall and the chairs.

Now Khanum Jan was standing close by. Ming asked me the meaning of the songs, which, as usual, he explained to his friends. Since Khanum Jan was a charming conversationalist, the guests spoke to her, too, off and on. While dancing around, she came to the four-sided container and scooped up a handful of cardamoms and other ingredients which are taken with the betel-leaf. She distributed them among the guests and hurled one betelnut at me. It fell in my lap. I tossed it in my mouth. Ming observed the little drama. I was scared. Khanum didn't care and continued to dance although she, too, knew that Ming had noticed her playful gesture.

She flung several betelnuts towards me. They fell down on the floor. One struck the fancy lamp placed on a teapoy. The fragile glass was cracked.

The sound attracted everybody's attention.

"What is the matter, girl? Why are you being so childish?" Mirzai scolded her.

"Khanum Jan, you will destroy my glassware," bewailed Ming.

She cocked a snook at him and demanded to know, "Did you understand the couplet?"

"What does it mean, Hasan Shah?" the poor man asked.

Suddenly she broke into another lyric which said *"Her face glows all night, surrounded, by black tresses... How bold is the thief, herself carries a lamp!"*

She laughed aloud and insisted that I explain it to Ming. The meaning was fairly obvious. I said, "She is talking about herself! See how boldly she smashed your lamp!"

In the morning Ming Saheb sent for the sedan chair. I got worried. I had not yet had its window repaired. Now he would shout at the bearers and blame me for negligence. Right then Tika Ram, the footman, appeared with the message that Saheb would like to see me.

Khanum Jan and Bi Jan were sitting smugly in Ming Saheb's parlour when I got there. I realised that Khanum Jan was up to some mischief again.

"Munshi," Ming said, "You do not take proper care of my things. Somebody in your house took a shot at the window panes of my *boocha*. I bought it only a month ago for six hundred rupees."

"Yes, Sir," I replied. "I noticed the damage and I was going to get it fixed when you sent for it."

"Khanum wants to go to the river to take the air."

My guess was right. I said aloud:

"She can go. The broken glass would be no hindrance to her gaddying about."

"How was it broken, anyway?" she asked peevishly.

"I have no idea, Madam." Then I addressed Ming. "When I was taking a nap in the afternoon, I had this dream in which I saw that I was in the litter, coming home from the riverside. As I approached my house I saw these Jan females. Khanum said to me, 'Why are you using my sedan chair? Saheb has given it to me.'

" 'Fair enough,' I answered, 'As long as I use it, the *boocha* is mine. When you take it, it's yours.'

"Upon which she got very cross and threw something at me. Luckily I wasn't hit, but the glass was smashed to splinters."

The Saheb knew I was joking. He said with mock gravity, "Well, Khanum Jan, you are the culprit." He caught hold of her hand jovially. "I won't let you go till you get it mended."

She freed her hand with a jerk and snapped, "Only you and your Munshi are truthful. Why don't you confess that your petty clerk does not want me to use the litter. If I knew it belonged to him, I would not have mentioned the damn thing."

"Why are you so worked up? We were merely teasing you. Take it easy. Hop in and go," said Ming gently.

"It's got very late. I will go tomorrow." She rose to her feet and left the room.

I was surprised again. Why did she persist in insulting me before Ming? What was the matter?

At night about a dozen Englishmen came to dinner and Ming entertained them to her song and dance. While dancing she again picked up some cardamoms from the bronze container and distributed them to the guests. She came towards me singing the last line—

Hafiz, be patient, and bear with me the hardships of days and night. Eventually you will succeed.

She went on to the next song:

Look, the bulbul has a crow in her nest...!

She smiled at me and said to Ming, "In England all your crows are white and they come to India, too!"

Poor Ming said simply, "Yes, we have white crows too."

I said, "Saheb, she is hitting at you. She is calling you white crows."

"You call us crows, Khanum Jan!" Saheb repeated sadly.

The audience roared with laughter.

O Candle of the Night of Excellence, Rose of the Garden of Attraction, I wrote to her the next day and complained of her various cruelties.

She wrote back....

O Chief of the Circle of the Wounded, Head of the Band of Restless Lovers...after which she explained her position.

One day I took some papers to Ming Saheb and he gave me a document to copy. I sat down at the table. As I began to work, Ming paced to and for with another Englishman.

Bi Jan and Khanum Jan dropped in. The English visitor left.

Ming picked up Bi Jan. He plonked down on a sofa chair, and made her sit in his lap.

I pretended to remain engrossed in the accounts. Khanum Jan came over and asked, "Hey, what are you doing?"

"Salaries."

"Lemme have a look." She took the sheet and began to glance at it.

"Look at the fun and games going on here. Give us a kiss, too," I whispered.

"Saheb, your Munshi is being very cheeky," she cried and placed her thumb on my lips. Ming saw it and said,

"What is it, Khanum Jan?"

"Your clerk is being naughty."

"What did he say?"

"I picked up this sheet of paper and asked him about it. He said, 'Run along. You have no business to be here. Saheb did not accept you. Won't even talk to you. Don't disturb me.'

"I was furious and sort of slapped him."

"Aren't you afraid of Hasan Shah, my dear?" Ming asked amiably. "He holds his peace because of me and you become naughtier by the hour."

"I also keep quiet for your sake," Khanum shot back.

He guffawed and said, "You were right, Hasan Shah, that it was sensible of me to let her go. But she keeps telling me that she rejected me."

"Huzoor, let it be, I will say nothing although I am livid."

"Take your revenge!"

"Thank you. Just tell her to leave me in peace."

"Khanum Jan, you should not have been so rude to him. Do you know how much he hates you?"[1]

After some more cantankerous dialogue she left in a huff.

Next time when she came to the bungalow she announced:

"Saheb, I am going to file a suit against him. It is a case of murder."

"What happened now?" Ming smiled expansively.

"I dreamed last night that this fellow came out of his cottage with a pistol in hand.

---

1. Urdu translator's note: Hasan Shah and Khanum Jan had their lovers' quarrels but this Saheb Bahadur was quite a clown, the way he barged in all the time. Alas such Englishmen do not come to India any more!

"In an instant he shot at me. I fell down, crying: 'Alas, alas, Khanum Jan has been killed.' I wanted to send you the bad news, when I woke up. Now kindly tell your stupid agent that because he did me in, he ought to pay me the compensation."

"The Munshi would not be amused. He does not like such jokes."

"Since I shot her in her dream, she should get the compensation in the same state of slumber. On the spot...where the crime was committed!" I put in.

An argument followed. Gravely she repeated her demand.

"I think she has become greedy for money, which is a characteristic of the women of her class. They are all gold-diggers," I blurted out.

Her face flushed. Shocked by my remark, she went back to her camp at once.

That evening she did not appear behind the tent-screen. I called Rahmullah. The brat was not available. I was perplexed by her warlike nature and her inexplicable tantrums. Rahmullah arrived the next day. I asked him why his foster-sister did not come out last evening.

"She says that you had uttered something abominable about her, in front of Ming Saheb. I will take my revenge, she says."

I folded my hands and begged of her to forgive me when I saw her shadow behind the curtain. The silhouette disappeared.

She began taking her music lessons after sunset and asked Mirzai to send for Ming. When he went into the tent she drove him crazy asking him the meaning of various ghazals. In desperation he sent for me.

"Yes, please call him," said Mirzai. "He never comes here on his own."

"He is diffident and bashful," answered Ming.

Tika Ram came twice to my place. Eventually, I had to go. "Why did you call me, Sir?" I asked my employer.

"Why not? What's the problem? Why don't you come here when these people invite you?"

"You know, Sir, I am not used to frequenting bordellos."

"I know that. But there is no harm in coming here. You won't lose your dignity."

I sat down next to Khanum Jan and whispered, "What is this new racket you have started?"

She didn't answer and began to sing. When she reached the couplet:

Hafiz, do not be sorrowful if the autumn winds blow across the garden. Think soberly: which rose does not have a thorn?

she repeated it, looked at me, and said to Ming, "It is true. No rose is thornless!"

"Quite right," he replied thoughtlessly. Then the significance dawned on him, and he complained:

"You call me a thorn!" He clasped her hand in feigned annoyance. She shook him off. Everybody laughed.

The women sang many soulful lyrics. I was deeply moved. So was Ming. He saw the tears in my eyes and said, "I am sure you are in love. Whichever of these women you like, take her!"

"That indeed would be our good fortune, Sir," Mirzai remarked.

"Saheb", I pleaded,' "I have requested you many a time not to indulge in ribaldry with me. You are my master and should not be so informal with your employee."

"What's wrong in it? Whenever you hear them sing, your eyes well up."

"Mir Saheb is merely an emotional and soft person. His tears have nothing to do with any love affair, real or imaginary," Mirzai said, with conviction.

"That's right. I just happen to be a sentimental fool. Alas, my tears are not effective!" I said lightly.

Saheb looked at the clock and rose from the chair. I stood up, too.

"Where are you off to? Please stay awhile," said Mirzai.

"I have a lot of official work to attend to," I replied solemnly.

"What kind of official work do you do at this hour?" Ming interrupted me. "Why do you hurt their feelings? Stay back."

That was precisely what I wanted to do. So I sat down again. Khanum Jan went out pointedly, to sit under the awning. So I had to come back home, after a while.

However, I started calling on them every evening. If for some reason I was late, Mirzai would come near the curtain and call out. I would go there and play chess, *chausar*[1] and *ganjafa*,[2] or participate in *bait-bazi*.[3]

Khanum Jan remained aloof and formal in the presence of others. I apologised to her in writing for calling her a gold-digger.

She forgave me graciously and despatched the list of her promises for the future. She had mentioned these in an earlier letter: "We must clear any misunderstanding immediately and not wait for the other to apologise first. Always consult each other for everything. Never be

---

1. A game like Ludo played with cowries.
2. Traditional Indian playing cards.
3. Each participant recites a couplet and the next person must come out with another couplet which begins with the last letter of the second line of the couplet just recited.

secretive. Never tell lies. Never refute the spouse and take note of gossip. Always try to augment one's love. To become content with the state of feelings one has in the present, is not wise. One should not stop caring about the state of your emotions in the future also."

She ended the letter with space left for signatures: — Khanum Jan — Hasan Shah. I marvelled at her intelligence, duly signed and returned the "document" to her.

Now I was desperate to marry her at the earliest and wrote to her: "Dear one, you say that you are waiting for the right time for us to marry. Do you have to consult astrologers and Brahmins? Hurry up, or I'll die."

We continued to correspond through Rahmullah. Then one day she informed me that she would let me know as soon as she found the chance to carry out our plan. I was pleased beyond words. She appeared behind the curtain, smiled, and went back. I gave five rupees to Rahmullah.[1] He declined to accept the tip. I was infuriated.

"Every time I give you a tip you refuse. Has Khanum Jan told you not to take any money from me?"

"She hasn't," he answered. "But if I take money from you I'll have to give it to my parents. They would ask me from where I got it. What would I say? I am not an independent adult. And I do not have any requirements. If I need a pice or two to get something for myself from the bazaar, I get it from Khanum Jan. In fact, she gives me so much pocket-money that I have really got fed up. And ever since I have become your go-between, she gives me five pice daily. So tell me, what more do I need?"

I said to myself: Khanum Jan is clever but this little imp is over-smart. As they say, even the mice in the Town Kazi's household happen to be full of wisdom!

---

1. Urdu translator's humorous note: "Earlier he had given two rupees. Now five. What generosity!"

However, the good news refreshed me. I regained my lost colour. My relatives were happy to find me hale and hearty. I gave charity to the poor. But after a week I became restless again. There was no news from her. Had she forgotten about me? What could the matter be? Then I received from her a lyrical letter full of hope and good cheer. It was written in rhymed prose. It revived me. In the morning she came near the screen and said: "Keep your bungalow empty tonight and get hold of four or two men."

"Why?" I asked.

"They are required for something."

I said, fine and asked Rahmullah, "Do you have some function at your place tonight?"

"Not at our place. The initiation ceremony[1] of Mewa Jan's daughter is to be celebrated today. Our folk are getting ready to go there."

"Khanum Jan too?"

"Yes, of course, because that girl is a close friend of my sister."

Strange. If she is going to a party why has she ordered me to keep the cottage vacant? I hope she is not out to hoodwink me again. Anyway, under some pretext I told my younger brothers (who often stayed with me) to go to Jajmau, where my grandpa lived. All day long that extraordinary girl remained engrossed in her make-up and so on.

---

1. The day a courtesan's virgin daughter was initiated into the profession, she was dressed like a bride. Her first patron removed her nose-ring and replaced it with a 'nose-flower'. The ceremony was celebrated like a wedding, to which all members of the courtesan's caste were invited for an all-night feast of music and dance. The expenses of the function were borne by the 'initiator', who was often the richest bidder for the coveted occasion. The rite was called missi which meant that for the first time the girl applied black paint called *missi* over her gums. It was one of the sixteen adornments of traditional Indian make-up.

She put on her dress and jewellery, braided her hair and made herself gorgeous. But when the time came to leave, she lay down on the bed and covered herself with a quilt. She complained of a headache and nausea. She was feverish and vomitted a little.

Mewa Jan's servant arrived with the carriage. Mirzai sent the other women along and stayed back to give Khanum Jan her medicine. After a few hours, Khanum Jan said, "Feeling better! But I am too weak to get up. You must go! Mewa Jan and we all belong to the same caste and profession. You ought to go. Apologise on my behalf. Nobody could be happier than me on this occasion. I will join you all there if I can, later tonight if I feel up to it. Otherwise, I will come in the morning."

Mirzai left Rahmulla's mother and Zafran, the maid, to look after the patient and went away. She kept sending a servant every half hour to find out about her ward's condition. After a while Mewa Jan herself came to see her. Khanum Jan told her that she was feeling sleepy and would feel better after a little snooze. Thus she got rid of Mewa Jan, too.

I was growing more restive and anxious because of the delay. In the evening I called four humble, indigent Muslims, gave them dinner and told them to stay a while saying, "Somebody is getting married here tonight. After the registration[1] is over, you can go." Late at night I tiptoed to the outer curtain of the tent. Her bed was close by. Come along, I whispered.

She arrived in the cottage and inquired about the four witnesses.

"They are here."

"Place the candle in your bedroom. I will wait there."

---

1. Muslim marriage is a civil contract, witnessed by four or two adult men.

She went in and sat down on the fourposter. I called the men in, fixed the dower money, and read out the solemn phrases of "Offer and Acceptance". The legal procedure was witnessed by the four men. I gave them some sweetmeat and cash and bade them goodbye.

It was not feasible to stay here, so I spent the night in her tent, and returned home at daybreak.

Mirzai arrived with the sun, and found Khanum Jan to be still quite feverish. She said, "I am all right. You should have come after all the ceremonies were over. After all, they are our colleagues and sisters-in-profession. They would mind." Mirzai agreed and went back. She returned with the rest of the gang at sunset.

Khanum Jan's temperature had gone up. Her face was flushed. Mirzai called me and whined, "In my absence you didn't bother about our Khanum. Look how poorly she is. Please get some prescription from your grandfather."

I said I will send her some medicine mixed with keora water. It would refresh her.

Khanum Jan was up and about in a couple of days.

My visits to the tent became more frequent but we were extremely cautious about keeping our marriage a secret.

Sometimes when I became a bit careless she reminded me, and said, "Now you should become more chummy with these females so that they have absolutely no suspicion about my relationship with you. Let each one of them imagine that you are interested in her. Even Mirzai. Despite her middle age, she is quite a flirt."

"I can't become a mercenary."

"You must learn some diplomacy. It will help eventually."

"You might get really suspicious!"

"I am not so foolish!"

So I began flirting with all of them. One moonlit night as we sat outside, Mirzai went in because of the heavy dewfall. Khanum Jan and the others also got up and left. Only Bi Jan remained. Suddenly she flung herself at me. Just then Khanum Jan returned and hastily retracted her steps. I hissed to Bi Jan, "Keep away lest Khanum Jan sees us."

"Let her. How does it matter? She is not going to confiscate any estates of mine if she does see us. Who the hell is she anyway?"

Perhaps Khanum Jan overheard all this. She came back and sat down smiling as though she had not heard or seen anything.

I felt awkward. Bi Jan looked embarrassed too. I got up and came away to my cottage.

The following night Khanum cornered me.

"So you had a good time with Bi Jan, hadn't you?"

I wanted to tell her the truth but she would have become more irate. "It was just light-hearted fun," I faltered. "Quite so," she said. She must have overhead Bi Jan's words. I should have told her myself. But she seemed to be riding a winged horse because as soon as she had spoken she vanished.

The next afternoon when I visited them she looked like a fury, eyes flashing, faced crimson with anger.

On the third day when I went there I found Mirzai sitting under the awning. She was blackening her gums with *missi*. I pulled up a chair near her.

"If you don't come for a couple of days we miss you," she said.

Suddenly my glance fell on my wife. She was also there busy beautifying herself with *missi*. Then she placed the mirror in front and combed her hair and chewed a betel-leaf. Zafran brought the pot of ground henna leaves and asked her if she would like to redden her soles, too. I noticed she had already reddened her palms.

"Mir Saheb, you look tired," Mirzai remarked.

"I have not been too well lately," I replied.

Somebody came. Mirzai began to talk to him. I turned my chair towards Khanum Jan. She smiled. I got up and cast the shadow of my head over her feet, as though to ask forgiveness. She stamped her feet and said to the maid, "Let's go in."

"It is so pleasant out here. Why do you want to go in? It is stuffy inside."

Khanum Jan slapped her and kicked the bowl of henna.

Then she looked at me and smiled again.

Strange girl.

We went in. Instruments were being tuned. Then they began to sing.

In the evening she said, "I saw with my own eyes what went on between you and that slut. I am not angry with you but I am furious with that bloody whore."

Our love for each other was so overwhelming that one day I fell off the horseback and hurt my right arm. Ming got me home in a palanquin. The same day Khanum Jan fell down in the garden and hurt her elbow. One day an insect got into my eye. Khanum Jan too had pain in her eyes.[1]

On a pitch-black night of the rainy season, I was asleep in my verandah when I dreamed that there was cloudburst, storm and lightning and I was sitting on the bed. The Faithful One had come out of her tent and stood in the rain. I called her. But she did not move. Lightning was about to

---

1. Urdu translator's comment: These were mere chance happenings. To call them the proof of overpowering love is silly.

strike. I wanted to rush out and fetch her when I woke up. It was pouring with rain. I covered myself with a thick bedsheet and went to sleep again. I had the same dream again. I woke up with a start and looked at the tent. In the flash of the lightning, I did see someone standing near the curtain. Suspecting a thief I picked up my revolver and looked out. The shadow remained motionless. I wondered if my dream was true. I ran out barefoot and found that it was indeed Khanum Jan. She was drenched and shivering. I brought her to the verandah. I made her take off her saffron dress which she had worn in the evening and covered her with a quilt. Then I made her wash her feet. I could not light a fire to warm her because my brothers were sleeping in the house. I gave her some cloves to chew. She said, "You didn't come in the evening, so I came out for a walk and reached the verandah. Here I found you asleep. Just then it started raining. I didn't feel like disturbing you, though I was very scared standing there in the rain."

Back in the tent at daybreak she woke up Zafran and said that she had got up at night to go to the bathroom but her foot had slipped and she had fallen down in the slush. She had a hot bath and changed, and went off to sleep.

When the people got up in the morning Mirzai said,

"What is the matter? Khanum Jan didn't get up for her morning prayers?"

Zafran narrated to her the cock-and-bull story the young woman had told last night. Mirzai went over to her bed and felt the pulse. Khanum Jan had again had high fever.

Ming and I went to see her. A carriage was sent to bring my grandfather from Jajmau. She recovered after ten days.

Now it happened that Ming's cook called Imam Bakhsh met Khanum Jan one day when she was taking a stroll. He salaamed her. Being a very polite person, Khanum Jan spoke to him with kindness. The rascal got the wrong idea. Azamji was friendly with the entire domestic staff. The cook put a gold ring studded with rubies inside a brocade purse full of scented betelnuts and presented it to Khanum Jan. In his letter he expressed his impatience to meet her.... The lady kept those things with her and through Mohammad Afzal she let him know that these gifts would be placed before Ming Saheb, along with the news that the frog had also started sneezing.[1]

The blighter was terrified. Now he wondered how he would be punished, if those things were not returned to him.

Rahmullah heard all this from Mohammad Afzal and recounted to me.

I was very unhappy. As dusk fell I found Rahmullah on the way to the tents. I accompanied him and found Khanum Jan wearing that ruby ring. I felt as though somebody had set me afire. Evil suspicions crossed my mind. Why didn't she mention this matter to me? There was certainly more to it than met the eye.

I didn't go to the tent the next day, nor the day after that, till Rahmullah came to call me.

Khanum asked me the reason for my absence.

"I have been pondering over that matter of the Cook and the Courtesan."[2]

"What the hell do you mean?"

"You did not even care to tell me."

"What was there to tell? It was such a small matter. I took care of it myself. Shall I get him here? Do you want to speak to him?" She summoned Rahmullah.

---

1. An Urdu proverb.
2. Urdu Translator: In this incident the author has revealed how extremely foolish he is.

The cook came, trembling with fear. He abjectly begged forgiveness. "Please do not mention it to anybody, otherwise I am done for," he whined. I assured him and asked what Khanum Jan had said to him.

"She was very angry, and said your present will be placed before Ming Saheb, tomorrow," he quaked

I was satisfied. But when Rahmullah came to my place in the evening he was chewing some cardomoms and perfumed betelnuts. "From where did you get them?" I asked.

"The cook had sent her these," he said innocently. "She distributed them to everybody and gave me my share."

I lost my temper again. I snatched the nuts and cardamoms and threw them on the floor. Then I proceeded to box his ears. The child started crying. He ran off to see Khanum Jan, and complained that Munshiji spanked him for no reason. "What was my fault?" he asked.

She sent him back to fetch me. He also brought the message that tomorrow morning she was going to give me a bit of her mind in the presence of Mr. Ming.

I grew more furious and told the boy that I will not go to see her. Why should I?

I didn't visit the camp in the evening, too. At night when I calmed down a little, I thought I really should not have slapped the little fellow. He was not to be blamed. He had told me the real story, and I had come to know the facts. It was very unfair of me, indeed.

The next morning when the boy came, I asked him how she was.

"She is all right, "said he, "though she did not have her dinner last night, and is very quiet."

So I sent her a note: "My dear, it is difficult to fathom the depth of your love for me, that is why a little thing hurts.

And you came out with harsh words which hit me terribly... as the poet says: *Instead of children's pebbles rose petals should be flung at mad Mazhar, for he has a fragile temper...*

She wrote back:

"My very clever friend! Look, the nightingale is an unintelligent creature, but how he adores the rose which has nothing except colour and fragrance. Sometimes he even sacrifices his life for the flower.

"Human being is the finest of God's creations, just because of suspicion and or displeasure he gets annoyed and makes no use of his wisdom. It is not your fault. I just happen to be unfortunate. Anyway, whoever is at fault, please forgive me and forget about it. Kindly send me some flowers from your garden. Today, I have put on a yellow dress[1] and would like to wear some flowers, too. If possible, come tonight. I promise you I will not say a word."

In the evening I met her in the makeshift courtyard of the camp. Sitting on a camp-chair, she bent down her head when she saw me.

I salaamed her gallantly and made her laugh.

She said, "Go in. I am coming."

I sauntered in and talked to Mirzai. After some mintues the others got up to go to their mess for dinner. Khanum said she was not hungry. After they had left, she flared up. "Why do you create such a fuss now and then? In front of others you are quiet and pleasant. Once I am out of sight, you start troubling me with your doubts and suspicions. And why did you beat up the poor boy? You behaved as though you did not even know me. Why? Don't you realise what kind of people I am trapped with? If you continue to create problems for me, I don't know how long our hush-hush marriage would last."

---

1. Springtime when the mustard blooms, Indian women wear yellow dress and celebrate the season.

"First you sent me a nasty reply. Secondly, I thought if you had not been kind to that rascal, the cook, he would not have given you a present. Not only that, you merrily distributed his cardomoms etc. amongst your folk. You should have told Mr. Ming and got him punished straight away."

"I am sure you are more intelligent than me. Don't you understand that the mere threat of hauling him up before Mr. Ming terrified him? After that to tattle to his Master would have been very petty on my part. I cannot make a mountain out of a mole hill and became a butt of jokes. His greatest punishment was that his ruby ring was not returned to him. Monetary loss is enough chastisement for a swine like him. And for this your advice was not needed.

"It was not a matter of national or great financial importance that you should have been consulted, so that you could get up an army with cannons and swords. For no reason at all you created such a hoo-ha. But I do think Bi Jan has influenced your mind and you talk sarcastically so that you can put the blame on me and leave me. Or maybe the fact that I do not observe *purdah* and also I talk freely with Mr. Ming that is biting you. As you quote a poet, *Inside the wine glass too, the Daughter of Grapes remains unveiled, even though she has become very pious.*

"I used to think that it is because of your manliness and sense of honour that you did not like my way of living. Actually, it is something else.

"By the blessings of the Lord Prophet I am made of a different mettle or else was it possible that I remained chaste, living as I do with these vile people? Or if I were to have affairs, was nobody better available that I would fall for a cook? As God is my witness, I find it distressing to go about unveiled, especially if somebody apart from Ming speaks to me, I feel like dying.

"Despite knowing all this, you go on and on like this. I do not find it funny."

"I am sorry, I just couldn't help it when I spanked the boy," I said feebly.

Mirzai came back and we changed the topic. But what she had said about Bi Jan rankled me. I came home in a bad mood. She sent for me again. I didn't go.

The next afternoon her chit came: "Can't understand the reason for your latest grievance. It is no good lending your ear to my enemies. In case you want a decision, please come in the evening, otherwise remember that I will release myself from many of the conditions I had set myself for maintaining the bond of love. And then you will not be able to do anything about it."

I felt contrite and accepted the invitation.

Khanum Jan, Mirzai and Bi Jan were all busy singing together. They sang many ghazals. Later, Bi Jan started a Holi song:

The month of Phagun[1] has come, my love.
I will mix colours in the water and drench you
I will hit you with marigolds and bubbles,
I will tease you no end and when you are angry
I will pacify you again...

As we went out to sit in the courtyard, Mirzai called Khanum Jan for evening meals. She repeated that she had no appetite. Mirzai said that for the last two or three months the girl had had no appetite.

I said I would get her some medicine from Grandpa.

---

1. The festival of throwing coloured water is celebrated in March. There are special joyous songs on this occasion, as well as some classical melodies expressing the happy mood of the season.

7

I had thought that this year we would enjoy the time of flowers in freedom.
But when prisoners came out of the cage, Autumn had arrived.

Azamji's troupe remained in the service of Mr. Ming for nearly one year. Suddenly news came that his brigade was going to be transferred to the east. One day Ming said to Mirzai that he was going with his regiment to Calcutta. "If I come back soon I will call you all again. Otherwise, we will have to call it a day."

After a few days he asked me to pay them off and give two hundred rupees each to Khanum Jan and Bi Jan, and hundred rupees to Mirzai as *bakhshish*.

Khanum Jan and I were stunned. The time finally had come for us to part. In the evening, I found them all together when I visited them in their large tent. The place which used to be full of merry laughter and song, was utterly quiet. Everybody was grief-stricken, as though a caravan had been robbed or somebody had died. The silence was funereal. As they left for dinner, my Moon-Faced One said, "This is the Doomsday I was dreading. But I had heard that the troops would leave next year."

"Don't despair. The transfer may be postponed or Bi Jan may get employment with the officer commanding of the new regiment."

"I cannot be convinced by these useless words. If you want us to remain together, find a way out, or you will lose me for good. Hurry up and do something," she said urgently.

After a few days Azamji decided that it was futile to wait here for the new army. It would only mean more expenditure. It was best to leave for Fort Chunar and join

Mr. Hollier there. He had "covered Bi Jan's head."[1] Probably he would engage her again.

They began looking for a boat. The same evening Khanum said to me, "What is to be done now?

"I had married you as a shelter and a haven for life, otherwise, I had decided never to get married. If Azamji etc. insisted that I lead a licentious life, I would have just killed myself, although it would have been a sinful death.

"Look at my bad luck. Now my meeting and marrying you already seems a dream. I am worried about my safety. These people may do anything when they reach their destination. Once I saved myself through my cunning, and even got their salaries fixed for their maintenance. This sort of thing cannot happen everywhere." She broke down.

"If you say I will put my life on stake for you and take you away from here."

"How can I tell you to endanger your life and honour for my sake? Think of something sensible, otherwise not yours but my life would certainly be lost."

"What shall I do?"

"Get hold of a pair of good horses....Your relatives and mine are not so rich as to mount a massive hunt for us. They would try a little and give up. Gulbadan ran away and these people did nothing. They did not even go a few miles out of Cawnpore to look for her."

So for a few days I secretly tried, and failed to obtain a pair of horses.

After their retrenchment the troupe had been very despondent. But ever since they had started searching for a boat they had become quite hunky dory. Mirzai used to cheer me up with her singing. Khanum Jan sang

---

1. The uninitiated courtesan remained bareheaded till her first client "covered her head" with her mantle.

heartbreaking songs of separation. Mirzai guessed that I had some kind of an emotional involvement with somebody. She tried to console me. Khanum Jan used to very cleverly say, "That is the reason why I didn't become friendly with him. For one day we were to part company. Bi Jan, dear, you tried to entice him but he retained his sense of proportions, otherwise today he would have been sighing, too."

One night when both of us were alone, Khanum Jan took out her jewellery box and said, "I will take this with me."

"If you do, this gang will surely chase you because of the ornaments."

"All right. Whatever they gave me, I will leave behind. What my mother had left for me, I will take along."

"Show me your own stuff."

She placed her personal jewellery before me.

"First of all, you should not take anything with you. If you insist, just take this diamond necklace, the thumb-mirror *arsi*, the rope of pearls. Also these emerald ear-leaves, and emerald rings. Keep them aside. I will take with me two hundred guineas and two hundred rupees. What I mean is, few valuables would not be noticed, and we can carry them on horseback. Only I have not yet found the horses."

"What else have you managed to do?" she asked with a sardonic smile.

"Azamji had booked a Dacca-style "Lovelock"[1] barge. I should take a small Bulwark. It has fast speed. After the Lovelock sets sail, I will follow it after three hours and overtake it. You hop on from your boat to mine, when you get a chance, and I will bring you back here. I will hoist a

---

1. English names used in the text.

chequered sarong atop the masthead, so that you recognise my vessel. When they come to know about your disappearance during the voyage, they would keep quiet.

"I have asked a friend to keep his house ready for us in Jajmau."

"Why don't you take me to Jajmau right away from here?"

"Because then our secret may be out and these people may get you back. If you change horses in midstream, they can't sail back to Cawnpore. They will have to wait till they reach Chunargarh, and then begin looking for you."

"Done! They are sailing on Friday. You reserve a boat now."

I engaged a Dacca-style "bulwark" and hired ten oarsmen, packed a hamper with foodstuff and fruit and sent a servant aboard.

Then I got busy with my office work. Ming told me that the accounts had not been cleared for the last five months. "The money-lenders have not been paid back and I have to leave soon," he grumbled.

I was worried. How would I be able to cope with so much work in such a short time? I decided to hand over the logbooks to my brother, Hussain Shah, and leave on the pretext of going to Jajmau.

As it happened, the troupe had to perform at several English officers' farewell parties. Their own departure was delayed by ten days. This respite was most welcome. I finished my work and asked Ming to check the ledgers. He said, "I am busy for the next two days, and tonight Mirzai etc. are coming. You will have to wait."

I met Mirzai in her tent.

"Yes, we have been rather busy with these concerts, and have put off our departure," she answered breezily.

Khanum Jan was also getting ready for the mujra.

"Very busy with the mujras and I don't even know!" I commented sourly. "My bad luck!"

"I don't do anything on my own. Whatever I do it is due to some compulsion or expediency. Why didn't you come there?"

Mirzai joined us and said, "You have cast a spell over us! We hate parting from you. If we didn't have to go in search of our livelihood, we would not have left this place."

My wife said dryly, "Why do you flatter him so? Not to see him again is not the end of the world. Once out of sight nobody is remembered. One should not indulge in hyperboles."

"What a bad-tempered girl she is!" Mirzai snorted. "Mir Saheb has been so good to us. We ought to be grateful." She left in a huff.

I said, "Why do you quarrel so, my good women? I am nobody. Why should anyone remember me? Don't be cross, Khanum Jan. Go ahead and forget me, wholesale!"

"I hate to be hypocritical."

"Whenever I would think of him, I would remind you of him, too!" said Bi Jan.

"Indeed?" Khanum merrily exclaimed.

Mithoo arrived with the message that Saheb had summoned all of them.

They got up to get ready. I returned to my cottage and arranged the cut-glass phials of Indian perfumes which were to be offered to the guests. Then I sent the perfume box to the bungalow.

After that Tika Ram came to call me.

Many ghazals were sung that night with the theme of parting. Everybody was moved. A newly arrived

Englishman gave five guineas to Khanum Jan in appreciation of her song.

Next morning was a Thursday. Mirzai and her colleagues went to the big house to say goodbye to their benefactor.

He said to me that after lunch he would have a look at the papers. In the evening I visited the tent. Mirzai asked me to stay for dinner. I politely declined. As they went to the kitchen-tent to eat, Khanum Jan asked me, "What was it Ming Saheb was saying about papers?"

"The bankers have not been paid back. I have worked hard at the tally. He is to see the records tomorrow but that is the day when you are leaving. I am in a fix. What shall I do? I must explain the registers to Ming Saheb. It will take at least two days. During that time your vessel will have traversed only about forty to sixty nautical miles. I suppose there is nothing much to worry about."

She sighed and said, "I hope that while you are involved here in the office accounts, the angels of death may not start taking my lifetime's account from me."

"Don't talk nonsense. I will finish the job in hand and catch up with you in no time."

"Hopefully. To me all this bodes no good. I think my days on earth are about to be over. The kind of luck I have, I do not expect to live a peaceful life. This is the hardest hurdle to cross. I can only see failures ahead."

"Nonsense!..."

I had just finished my dawn prayers when Mirzai and the others turned up at my cottage to say goodbye. They were weeping copiously. Khanum's eyes were dry. Her face had lost its glow and she seemed to be in a state of shock. Still, her composure was truly admirable.

I asked them to sit down. "This," I said "is precisely the reason why I did not want to become very friendly with you all, because then we would part with a heavy heart. And that's what has happened. I can't bear to think that you good people are going away."

They stayed for a short while. I accompanied them to the gate. Mirzai kissed my hands.[1] Khanum Jan remained a picture of grief and bade me a wordless farewell.

I shed many tears when I returned to the house. I had just said a very uncertain goodbye to my beloved wife.

After a few minutes the men arrived to take their leave. I bade adieu to Azam Jan, Azamji and the rest of them, and they left.

Little Rahmullah was the last to come. With his dog-like devotion for his foster-sister, he had been the woodpecker[2] and the carrier-pigeon for us, and he had shared my secrets. When I saw him, I burst into tears. He consoled me and said, "Khanum Jan says you have promised to come to Chunargarh. So we will all meet again!"

The sun came up. Ming sent for the damned inventory. I went to office to cast up accounts.

In the evening I came home and obtained the news from the river-port. I was told that Azamji's vessel had sailed in the afternoon.

The following day I was engrossed in my book-keeping when some Englishman sent a chit to Ming. He said to me, "I am going out right now. I will see the balance sheet tomorrow," and stalked out of the room.

That meant another day's work. I came home.

God damn it, my departure was delayed once again.

---

1. A gesture of veneration, for the author was a descendent of the Prophet.
2. According to Muslim legend a woodpecker carried the Queen of Sheba's letters to King Solomon.

The next morning I felt like decamping on the quiet.

Better sense prevailed, however. I went to the warehouse and worked till lunch time. I tried to close the books but it was not possible.

On the fourth day, I handed over the audited ledgers to Mr. Ming and requested him to give me another week to pay off the creditors. And finish the remaining work. I also told him that I would go to Jajmau and do all the monetary arithmetic, undisturbed at my grandfather's house. He permitted me to do so.

I repaired to my cottage and told my cousin Mohammad Yusuf that I was going to see Lala Tika Ram, for there seemed to be a mistake of several hundred rupees in the cashbook.

I gave my cousin two hundred rupees for household expenses and said, "Take care and do not postpone any important matter if it crops up in my absence. I will be at Mir Roshan Ali's place for the next two or three nights and shall see the Lala in the day time."

I told my khidmatgar and confidante, Hasan Ali, that I was going on an important errand, "Don't tell anybody that I am out of town."

After that I went to see Lala Tika Ram and talked shop with him. On Monday, after saying my afternoon prayers, I went off to the pier. I had taken a hundred guineas with me. My luggage was already aboard. Before embarking I told the crew that apart from their salary I would give them five rupees a day as bakhshish but they must cover two day's distance in one.

Up oars! They shouted and rowed away from Cawnpore. They worked very hard indeed, and on the third day we reached Kara Manakpur, near Allahabad.

When we set sail from there and arrived at the confluence of the Ganges and the Jamuna, the boatswain asked me which way to take, for the river forked from there. I told whichever way you see more traffic of the countrycraft, follow it.

I didn't give them a moment's rest. They navigated day and night till we reached Allahabad. Still, there was no sign of Azamji's barge.

The oarsmen said that even the fastest Lovelock ship would have not reached here so soon. "They left a week ago, on Thursday. We sailed after three days. That vessel cannot reach here in a week's time. It seems that from the confluence they took some other route, otherwise we would have met them on the way."

I was distressed beyond words and decided to go back to the fork and take the other route.

> *O camel-driver, halt, and see if this is not the forest of Nejd.*[1]
> *Why else did Laila's camel suddenly stop on the way?*

We turned back to take the alternate waterway.

Since the wind was not westerly, our speed was slow. The boatsmen punted with their bamboo poles or pulled the boat with ropes. We continued thus for another three days and yet could not spot Azamji's Lovelock.

My sailors informed me that Cawnpore was eighty miles from there. "Tell us where to go. We have been waterborne for ten days and have not espied the other boat. Now it is impossible to trace it."

I told them not to give up the chase.

> *I am lost in the flood of tears.*
> *My condition is worse than that of Noah.*[2]

---

1. Majnun, the legendary lover of Laila wandered in the desert of Nejd. (Arabia).
2. This is an Urdu couplet.

The captain turned eastward. Just before sunset the sailors moored the boat at a landing stage, in order to take a little rest. I went ashore and began walking up and down the embankment. I noticed that other watercraft had also stopped there recently, for some litter was lying on a side. I strolled over and found a piece of paper tied to a bit of driftwood. I opened it quickly and saw a familiar handwriting. I kissed it and began reading with bated breath....

"My Indifferent One, may you live long! Ever since I bade adieu to you and my boat got stuck in the whirlpool of exile, I have been waiting for you every moment, day and night. My eyes have started watering as I continue to gaze at the watery expanse. My neck aches as I keep looking back hoping to catch a glimpse of your vessel. Our own ship keeps rocking because of the strong gales. I become dizzy and sick. I have been looking for you for the last six days. Your boat has become the Crescent Moon of Eid. I stare around with wide eyes but it just cannot be sighted. It seems that my boat of life has become storm-tossed. I am feeling giddy. Stars are falling and breaking into my eyes. You are still worried about those blasted files and documents. You have lost your own ship of freedom and I am half-dead here, and how anguished! I am sure you must be enjoying yourself with your cronies at home. I have grown weak because I cannot eat or drink anything. I am too sick for words. Try to come so that I see you before I die....

Thursday, 7th Jamadiul Sani."[1]

I was beside myself with grief. My servant tried to console me. The captain climbed the gangway and said, "Sir, we did our best, but failed in our mission. What shall we do now? We are here to follow your orders. We don't know Lovelock's whereabouts."

---

1. Seventh month in the lunar Islamic calendar.

"I do not know at which inauspicious moment I had boarded this vessel. For the last eight days I have been scanning the waters, to no avail," I replied ruefully.

It was futile to continue the search. If we see them near Chunargarh I may not get the chance to carry out my plan of boat-to-boat rescue. If I disembark at Chunargarh, I may not be able to take her away with me. And apart from returning home without success, it will take another twenty days to sail back to Cawnpore. I wish I had followed them immediately after their departure. Now all that is a dream and I have nothing in store except ridicule and failure. There is no alternative except going back to Cawnpore. After finishing all my chores, I will set out again to bring back my dear wife. Then I could face all eventualities. I will do whatever I can to bring her back from Chunargarh.

Luckily, an easterly wind rose and the masts were taken off. The boat gathered speed. That day we traversed sixty nautical miles. The next day, too, the wind was favourable, and by late afternoon we reached Sarsia Ghat, Cawnpore. I paid off the boatmen and went straight to Lala Tika Ram. From there I made for home. On the way I met my khidmatgar, Hasan Ali, who told me that everybody had been frantically looking for me for the last two days.

I went to see Ming and said, "I had told you that I will go to Jajmau, and work there in peace. Yet you mounted a regular search for me!"

"You have never remained absent for so long. I did wait for you first, then tried to find your whereabouts. The staff must be paid their salaries; so many things have to be sorted out," he replied.

I duly performed my duties, and after a couple of days I travelled to Jajmau to meet my folk. On my return I decided to send a courier to Chunargarh to get some news of Azamji. After that I thought, I would do what had to be done about the rescue of Khanum Jan.

8

I have seen the mounds under which the Rose Faced
Ones are buried.
Look, this is how those who must die, pass away...[1]

I was still thinking about sending the messenger, and one day I said to Ming, "I wonder if Azamji and company have reached Hollier Saheb's headquarters in Fort Chunar."

"I have already written to Hollier. I am waiting for his reply."

I thanked my lucky stars that now I didn't have to worry about sending my own messenger.[2]

More than a week passed but no reply came from Chunargarh. I reminded Ming. He said he would write again.

"Ask about Mirzai, etc., too," I put in.

"Are you concerned about them?"

"Mirzai had promised to write. Maybe they have gone somewhere else."

Saheb dashed off another letter.

The reply came after a week. Hollier had written to say:

"Azamji's troupe has arrived. I have employed Bi Jan on rupees one hundred per month. Unfortunately the climate out here did not suit Azamji's adopted daughter and she fell ill. A fortnight ago they took her to Lucknow for medical treatment.

I was terribly upset and made up my mind to proceed to Lucknow. But first I must send a letter to find out how she was.

---

1. Lines from Urdu ghazals.
2. Urdu translator's sarcastic comment: "that is how much he loved Khanum Jan!"

I was planning to despatch a man to Lucknow but somehow could not do anything about it. I spent sleepless nights and recited much doleful poetry to myself, till one day I did finally decide to send a *harkara* on Sunday. On Friday, however, there came a man with a letter from Mirzai, addressed to Ming. The other envelope was for my grandfather. She had informed the Hakim that on the way to Chunargarh Khanum Jan had fallen ill. When they reached their destination Bi Jan was engaged by Hollier Saheb. Many doctors were called for Khanum Jan. Prescriptions were changed but she got worse.

The bad climate aggravated her ailment. She grew very weak. "Eventually, we brought her to Lucknow. We are putting up at Bhim-ka-Akhara, near the English cantonment. Here, too, we have shown her to many well-known *hakims*. There is no improvement. She is growing weaker by the day. During our sojourn in Cawnpore when she was unwell you had very kindly treated her and she had always recovered. Now she has herself said that if the venerable Hakim Saheb comes here, God willing, I would be all right. Therefore, at her insistence I take the liberty of asking you to please come here. I am also requesting Ming Saheb to allow Syed Hasan Shah Saheb to accompany you. You will save Khanum Jan's life and we will become your slaves for ever."

The letter to Ming carried the same request. He asked me to call my grandpa.

When he arrived from Jajmau, Ming said to him, "Khanum Jan is a highly intelligent and talented young woman. I hope to God that she gets well. Do go across to Lucknow and see her." Grandfather agreed.

The courier met me alone at night and said, "The lad Rahmullah had given me a sealed envelope which I am to deliver to you."

"My Indifferent One! I am sure you must have followed me on the river but could not overtake our boat. I can't believe that your office work hindered you from coming. Anyway, hoping against hope, that you may sail past, I wrote two letters and tied them to some sticks on the landing stages along the waterway. Still you didn't show up, nor was there any news from you. Nothing happened. Now there is no hope. The angel of death is standing before me, saying: The climate of the world did not suit you. Come along!

"The people have probably already felt that I am about to leave.

"There is sorrow in the air. The roses have torn their garments of patience and are sitting in a row to grieve. The bulbuls are about to recite my elegy. The boughs are bent down in grief. Willows have started weeping. Cypresses stand still.

"Pine boughs are wringing their hands. The wind has spread a carpet of leaves for the mourners. How strange that when so much lamentation is in the atmosphere, it has had no effect on you! You have not even asked who's death is being mourned? Who has this day mingled unto dust?

"Even then I am not blaming you. Just now, I was carried away by emotions and penned these lines! Just an outpouring of my poor, overburdened heart. Please come before I die. It is a precept of our Lord Prophet that one must look after the sick.

"I am in Lucknow and have insisted on calling your grandfather here. Only so that you may come over too. And for that I will try to cheat Izrael for a few more days!"

After reading the letter I went to Grandpa and said, "I have always wanted to meet my Lucknow relatives. Can I come along too?"

"I don't mind, if Ming allows. I believe there is a lot of work for you to do here."

He asked Ming, who said, "The new regiment has already reached Allahabad. And there are a lot of things to sort out and wind up here. The day the new regiment arrives, I will leave. It would not be feasible for Hasan Shah to go at this juncture."

"I am not going to Lucknow to settle down there. I will return with Grandpa. And if he takes long, I will come back alone. I won't stay there for more than a week."

"All office work must be cleared first."

"I will do it on my return."

"No, you will do it now." He turned to Grandpa "Why is he so keen to go?"

So I had to stay for another three days to finish the damned work. Ming and Grandpa gave their letters to the messenger, telling Mirzai to wait for a few days. I handed over my letter with the instructions that it should be given to Rahmullah.

I wrote to Khanum Jan in detail about all that happened after she undertook her voyage. I assured her that I will be reaching Lucknow in three days' time.

The man left in the morning. Another messenger arrived in the afternoon. Grandfather asked him to stay back and accompany us to Lucknow. Meanwhile I finished the work. I was to leave on Thursday in the morning. The news of my impending departure brought droves of tradesmen etc. to the door, all demanding to be paid off right away. Further delay. We could not leave before sundown, and had to stay in Unnao overnight.

On Saturday evening we entered Lucknow. Grandfather told Mirzai's messenger that we were going to stay in the city, in Mahmood Nagar, at the house of Maulvi

Altaf Rasul. "Go and inform Mirzai that we have arrived. Come here tomorrow morning, and take us to the campoo."

"I am tired", the man said. "The cantonment is quite far from here. I will stay the night at your host's place and take you there in the morning."

At night when my grandfather and the Maulvi Saheb sat down to dinner I could not eat a morsel and went directly to bed.

At sunrise Grandfather got ready to go. "I will also come with you," I said.

"Come along. On the way back we will stop at your grandma's parental house."

We reached Azam Jan's place near Bhim-ka-Akara and found many people reciting the Holy Quran as they do on the third day of the burial. Azamji and Mirzai were shrieking and throwing dust in their hair in a frenzy of grief.

I had a momentary blackout but could not weep. Tears welled up in Grandpa's eyes.

Mirzai saw him and came towards us. She squatted down on the floor and wailed.

"Hakim Saheb, my little girl had to go. That's why your departure was delayed. I sent you courier after courier. But we were predestined to mourn her death and she was predestined to die young. She waited for you to the last moment of her life. She died in the morning. The previous night she asked me, 'Mother, when did you send the second messenger?' I said he left on Sunday and must have reached Cawnpore the same evening. She said, 'So if Hakim Saheb had left on Monday, he would have been here at the latest on Wednesday or Thursday. It is Thursday night tonight, and there is no sign of him. Perhaps Ming did not let him come. Well, it was God's will that I die with such profound unhappiness in my heart.' She wept and sighed and said, 'I am grateful to God that he preserved my honour and released me from a thousand troubles and miseries.'

"I said, 'Don't be so despondent. If Hakim Saheb doesn't come today, I will send another man. Do not worry, you will get well.'

"She said ironically, 'Yes, I should not worry. Everything points to my getting well and surviving. Yes, why, should I worry!'

"To the very last she was in full possession of her senses. She turned her face towards Mecca and recited her prayers and placed her forehead on her pillow in genuflexion.

"We were relieved a little. We had been awake for many nights. So we got up to have a little nap. After about three hours she called out to me and said, 'You have not eaten since the morning. Perhaps because of me none of you have taken your meals. Go and eat, and get some sherbet for me. I feel thirsty.'

"I mixed some keora in *bed mushk*.[1] She sipped a few spoons. We were happy that with God's grace she was feeling better. So we went in and had our meals. When I came back to her room I found her fast asleep. I was very pleased because she had not slept well for the last one month. In the morning she woke up and asked if it was time for dawn prayers. Seoti said: 'Yes, bibi, it is time for the prayer.'

"Khanum made her 'dry' ritual ablutions and said her prayers on her pillow like the previous night. Then she raised her hands and prayed aloud, 'O Almighty, You are Merciful. I am a sinner. You are Omniscient and You know what I had truly wished for and I had requested You to

---

1. "Willow Musk", extract of the willow bark.

fulfil my wishes, or at least keep me safe in the den of iniquity in which I was imprisoned. My wish was not fulfilled but You saved me from leading a sinful life, and did not let my modesty be outraged.'

"I was making my own ablutions for the morning prayers, when I overheard her words of Thanksgiving. I too thanked God that she had recovered.

"After my prayers, I began telling my beads. Then I went to her bedside to recite the Benediction to the Prophet and blowed the words on her face. When I removed the quilt from her forehead I sensed that she was not breathing. I felt her pulse. It had hardened, 'Bibi, Bibi', I uttered. There was no response.

"I fetched the lamp and saw her. Her soul had gone up to Heaven. The body had become lifeless.

"The world turned dark in my eyes. Everybody began to sob and scream...

"She was bathed and shrouded, and by forenoon the bier was ready. After the Friday service the congregation said her funeral prayers at Takia Shah Abdul Nabi. The shrine is adjacent to Bhim-ka-Akhara. There, in the cemetery that unique jewel, that Sun of Honour and Modesty went down in a grave for ever.

"The mourners came back with empty hands and dust-laden hair.

"Mir Saheb, how can I enumerate to you her countless qualities of head and heart? How lovingly I had brought her up! How do I find my Joseph[1] who is lost for ever? Which passing caravan shall I ask...?

"An ominous hour it must have been when we set out from Cawnpore. That proved to be the Last Journey for my darling child.

---

1. A favourite metaphor: Joseph was very good-looking.

"During the first three days of the voyage she was perfectly all right, although she did look pensive and gloomy, and did not eat at all. I thought that was due to the river-sickness which all of us were suffering from.

"On the fourth day she had high fever. When we reached Chunargarh she got worse. So we brought her to Lucknow. We consulted one hakim. He was no good. We called Hakim Mir Ali. Khanum said, 'I will only get well if you call Hakim Nawaz from Cawnpore.'

"Since you got delayed I sent for Hakim Shafai. But her days on earth were numbered. On Thursday night she said to herself, "Death seems to be round the corner, otherwise Hakim Saheb would have come.""

Grandpa went to the adjoining room to see Azamji. I broke down. Mirzai said bitterly, "Why do you cry now? It was because of you that Hakim Saheb got held up."

I went over to my grandfather and said, "These people have not eaten for the last two or three days. Please make them have their lunch."

They sent for some food. I came out and looked around for Rahmullah. He came running and flung his little arms around me.

Both of us wept. I wanted to go with him to the cemetery but someone appeared and said, "Your grandfather is calling you."

"You had promised to follow us on a boat," whispered Rahmullah.

"Yes, I had."

"That's why Khanum had taken a berth near a porthole and kept looking out at the river. She used to turn her head now and then to look back. She did not see Mirzai and Azamji for a couple of days. Just kept lying on her bunker or read Diwan-i-Hafiz or that little book of poetry you had given her. On the fourth morning when she woke up I went to say good morning to her, she looked extremely unhappy. Her eyes had become bloodshot as though she had been crying incessantly. She did not eat anything that day. In the afternoon she brought up the food she had taken the previous day. Everybody came in to see her. But she said nothing, only expressed her desire to be left alone. After they went out of the cabin, Zafran began to massage her soles. I rubbed the palms of her hands. She said, 'Did you see, Rahmullah, that Heatless One did not show up.'

"I guessed she was alluding to you, but because of Zafran's presence I could not ask her anything. Her fever began to increase and she had nothing except a few spoons of lentils and rice. After four days she said to me, 'Go and sit on deck and tell me as soon as you spot a small boat with a blue chequered sarong hoisted to its top mast.'

"So I began to spend all day upon the top deck, looking out for you.

"Every time our craft dropped anchor at a wayside *ghat*, Khanum Jan would get up to go ashore. She wouldn't listen to Mirzai and others, and walk down the gang-plank despite her weakness.

"During a stop, one afternoon, she asked me to get some branches from a tree, I did that. She said, 'Tie them together with a rope and install it like a pole in the sand. Then attach this letter to it.'

"I followed her instructions. She made me do the same thing for her second letter, near Allahabad.

"I did find her first letter tied to some sticks, at a landing stage," I told him.

"She grew worse in Chunargarh and said, "Take me to Cawnpore or Lucknow. The climate here is awful.'

"Although Bi Jan had been employed by Hollier Saheb, everybody had got very worried about Khanum Saheba. So we brought her to Lucknow. Many hakims were consulted but there was no improvement in her condition. So at her insistence a man was despatched to Cawnpore. She gave me a letter quietly to be delivered to you. The courier brought back your reply. She began to cry, and said, 'He could not come because he is so dutiful and loyal to Ming. Now I am sure he won't turn up.'

"I said, "Do not be disheartened. He will certainly come one of these days.'

"She said, 'I did not expect such infidelity from that cruel man. Or perhaps he is in such deep trouble that despite the knowledge of my grave illness, he could not make it. It must be those blasted accounts of his. From the beginning the accounts were dodging him. Because of those wretched ledgers our plans for the future came to nothing.'

"She waited desperately for you on Tuesday and Wednesday. On Thursday she got some water heated and had a sponge bath. She made herself ritually clean for prayer, changed her dress and ordered that nobody should come to her room for a while. Then she called me and said, 'Mix a little lime in water and bring the cup to me.'

"I did that. At the time of late-afternoon prayers she stitched a white paper inside a purse and said, 'If that Heartless One comes along with Hakim Saheb, give this to him. If he does not, do your best to send it to Cawnpore. This is my Will, and your last service to me. Your final duty.'

"I said, If God wills, he will come, otherwise I shall go to Cawnpore and bring you his reply.'

"She broke down and wept bitterly. 'My little brother' she said, 'Death has appeared in my vision. I can see the face of Izrael. Now all this is nothing but a dream.'

"I began to cry too and came out of the room."

"God damn the job which stopped me from coming.' I sighed. "Even if armies had barred my way, I should have staked my life to come here. Now it's too late." I heard grandfather's voice. He was calling me. "Look, I must leave. I shall come tomorrow, and go with you to the graveyard."

As we were leaving, Rahmullah quietly slipped the purse in my hands. On the way back to town I got off at my grandma's house.

There, when I got a chance I went into an empty room and opened the cloth envelope. A plain white paper emerged, with the following lines written on top: *Dip it in the blood of tears and ye shall know the secret of my epistle.*

I dipped the paper in water.

The words appeared. This was her final letter and was full of heartbreaking poetry and more heartrending descriptions of how she had waited for me, how much she had wanted to live and spend her life in conjugal bliss with me. In the end she had added: "You must bear the loss with fortitude, and not make a spectacle of yourself with lamentations, etc. I think for an honourable woman to die early is a boon from On High. It means that just as she remained aloof in her dignity while alive, she was taken away from the world early so that she could go behind the Veil of Eternity for evermore.

'...And in case you regret that you were unable to come to Lucknow, take it as the Will of God. You should not feel sorry and I must not complain. I also ask you, my faithful friend, never to fret and fume for nothing. And when you sit down to eat, always take out a little food for the poor and sprinkle a drop of water on the ground. Thus you will give peace to my soul and you will also remember me.

"Now I come to the end of this morbid letter. If I am to survive the illness, we will live happily thereafter. Otherwise, God be with you. I entrust you to His care...."

The next morning Grandpa came from Mahmood Nagar and picked me up from Granny's house. Together we went again to Azamji's place in the contonment. Mirzai began to talk about the departed. I slipped out and went to the cemetery with Rahmullah.

Dust is blowing, there is a crowd of loneliness—Look, that is the grave of someone you loved...[1]

I lost all control of myself and began to knock my head on the tombstone. I fell over her grave, embraced it, and shrieked. Soon I went berserk. I threw myself on the ground twice. Rahamullah tried to stop me but the third time when I hit the ground I went on rolling and slid into a pit.

The lower half of my body got entangled in the weeds and brambles which surrounded the cavern.

Rahmullah shouted for help. The sexton came running. Both of them pulled me out with great difficulty. In the struggle one of my shoes got left behind in that empty grave.[2]

Rahmullah fell at my feet and said, "Please, Sir, never behave so insanely again. It will be harmful to me. You will also get a bad name. And it is all so futile."

I had hurt my hip bone and was exhausted. I sat down and rested my head on her grave. Rahmullah began to give me a little massage. I groaned and wished I could die...How could I live without her? How...?

Rahmullah's massage soothed me a little and I fell asleep.

I saw Khanum Jan sitting on a divan, freshly bathed and wrapped in a bedsheet. Water dripped from her wet hair.

---
1. Lines from an Urdu ghazal.
2. Urdu translator's note: What a big loss!

I lay on the floor, face down. I said to her, "I was told that your enemies[1] were ill. I find you hale and hearty. Perhaps it was a pretext to call me to Lucknow!"

She said, "I was very ill indeed. The moment you came I recovered. But I dislike your stupid behaviour. You are so intelligent and yet so silly."

I said: "Sorry, couldn't help it. Somebody told me that your enemies had died...

"So, I went haywire and wanted to kill myself."

"Even if it were true, you did not keep the promise I had taken from you, not to grieve too much... Anyway, I am not dead. I am quite all right. If you behave foolishly again, I will not foresake my rights on you and on the Day of Judgement I will corner you[2]... Now you go, I have to change..."

I was about to say something when Rahmullah sneezed and I woke up from my reverie.

I rose to my feet, and recited the Benediction over her grave.

On the way back I narrated the dream to Rahmullah. He said, "Now I do not need to console you. She herself forbade you not to grieve too much."

I gave him ten rupees and said, "If your parents agree you can come and stay with me in Cawnpore. Otherwise, too, whenever you like, you can come over, if you need my help."

After nearly a week grandfather and I returned to Cawnpore. Mr. Ming was very sorry when he heard the sad news.

---

1. The ultimate in old-world Urdu politeness. It would never be said to somebody that you were indisposed. It would always be your enemies who were indisposed.
2. The legal rights a woman has on her husband, according to Muslim Personal Law.

I have followed her advice and leave a little food for the poor at every meal. and I remember her every day.

Although the essence of love cannot be defined by reason, the curtain of its inner chamber can be seen only by the discerning eye.

Maulana Jelaluddin of Rome[1] who is among the blessed says:

When one tries to explain the phenomenon called love one ponders over its quality and essence and one is faced with failure and embarrassment, because, love and falling in love can only be explained through love. Reason is totally helpless as its interpreter. When one talks of the reality of love, the pen breaks down and the paper is torn to shreds. O my love, remain happy and ever successful, because thou art the physician of all my ills.

Love is superior in honour and unique in contentment. As for the matter of essence and qualities, Love's qualities are in its essence and the lover represents its splendour. Love's eternal beauty is of God and itself sings the song of love.

Love manifests itself in the two worlds, it is king as well as beggar. Hark! Love means the enjoyment of the agony. Anyone who wants to partake of the pleasures of life through it is far from the alley of love and loving. This handful of dust dare not say much about it, for a wanderer in the lane of love says:

All life long I wrote down the story of love. Life came to an end but the saga did not.

What you read just now is one such spectrum of tales, full of the marvels of fidelity and adoration. So, to quote a poet:

---

1. Please see notes.

From Naziri hear the vivid story of the Time of Flowers.
The anguished nightingale would narrate it to you.

With my distraught mind I have chronicled some of the events from my childhood upto the year 1203 A.H. (1787) and therefore I did not care to compose rhymed and ornate prose.

I have called this "a colourful story" and through the wordcraft of Taamia I have derived the year of its composition.

When Hasan finished writing this tale,
He asked Haatif[1] its period and date,
"Thank God, through the system of taamia,"
Quoth he, "This wondrous many-hued tale came to an end."
1205 A.H.

Praise be to God.
The narrative of love is my embellishment
Like the candle which contains fire in its tongue.
O God, give my pen the testimonial of popularity,
Like the sugarcane which fills one's mouth with sweet juice.
I want this narrative to be my memorial.
For life is a traitor.
Whoever reads this, please pray for me, because
I am a sinner.
O Lord, for the sweet sake of the Children of Fatima,
Let me die steadfast in the Faith.
O Allah, do not reject my plea,
For I am holding on to the corner of the Garments of the Children of Mohammed.
God bless him.

---

1. The Voice from Heaven.

Afterword

Not much is known about Hasan Shah's later life except that he left Kanpur and settled down in Lucknow. There he became a disciple of the famous poet Jurrat. Probably he never married and eventually lived like a faqir (mystic). He was alive when his younger brother Hussain Shah died in 1833. Hussain Shah had achieved considerable recognition as a poet and writer. (Also see notes)

The calligraphed manuscript of "Nashtar" was found in a private collection in Patna. Hasan Shah had called it simply "The story of Beauty and Love". "Nashtar" was the title given by Sajjad Hussain Kasmandavi.

Hasan Shah has remained more or less unknown.

With the publication of the present translation he makes his appearance, exactly two hundred years later, in 1991, in a different kind of India. Today, Cawnpore (now spelled Kanpur) is one of the largest industrial cities of the East, half-hidden in factory smoke. River traffic between Cawnpore and Calcutta gradually disappeared with the introduction of railways in mid-19th century. Picturesque Jajmau—where the Company's Englishmen had built their riverside bungalows—is now known for its tanneries!

Social attitudes have drastically changed due to the incessant efforts of reformers and pioneers. Right down to the early 1930's singing and dancing were considered the disreputable professions of *tawaifs* and *devdasis*. Today classical dance and music have become part of the education of an increasingly large number of middle-class girls. *Tawaifs* and *devdasis* have long vanished from the social scene, although we must remain grateful to them for having preserved and kept alive the finest traditions of India's classical dance and vocal music.

Women Writing in India was recently published by Anveshi, Hyderabad. The anthology includes extracts from Muddupalani's Telegu poem *Radhika Santwanam*. The author was a courtesan attached to Thanjavur court of the 18th century. Another learned courtesan Nagaratnamma published the book in 1910.[1]

In an anthology of the 19th-century women poets of Urdu and Persian published in the 1920's, the compiler made two categories: "ladies" and "entertainers." "Ladies" included princesses, high-born women and ordinary housewives. The entertainers comprised a large number of *tawaifs* including Eurasian and Jewish courtesans of Calcutta. A booklist of Naval Kishore Press of Lucknow once advertised a novel translated from English by "Mah-Munir, Chowdhrain of Lucknow." A chowdhrain was the head of the courtesans' guild.

Many learned courtesans held their own salons, attended by the most eminent poets and scholars of the day. In a society where the housewife was not supposed to step out of her courtyard, (they were generally uneducated, even illiterate), the courtesan provided intellectual company to male elite. This was exactly in the tradition of ancient India where the *vaishya* was required to know all the fine arts, and be a perfect companion of men. Japanese wives still do not accompany their husbands to parties, and geishas continue to entertain the men. The *devdasi* or temple dancer of the South held a similar position with her refinement and education.

---

1. Meenakshi Mukherjee, *The Times of India*, Sunday Review, August 1, 1991.

The high-class *tawaifs*, literally tramps, were called tent-dwellers, for they accompanied kings and generals on their hunting trips and wars.

After the Fall of Delhi eminent poets, scholars, artists, architects and musicians, all flocked to Lucknow and found lavish patronage at the new Court of the Nawab-Viziers of Oudh. Lucknow became the new cultural capital of north India for the next eighty years. As kingdoms go, it was a brief period and so the fairy-tale Sultanate can easily be called our Camelot. Khanum Jan died in 1787. The capital had recently been shifted to Lucknow from Faizabad and the city was yet to attain its full glory. Ruswa's *Umrao Jan Ada* was published in 1899. The latter also seems a real-life account of a courtesan of Lucknow. Khanum Jan stands at the beginning of Camelot, Umrao Jan witnesses its fall, and the end of a brilliant civilisation in 1857. Like Khanum Jan, Umrao Jan, too is very well educated, sensitive and highly intelligent. Hasan Shah was a romantic, old-fashioned youth, lamenting his fate and casting himself in the mould of the tragic lovers, Majnun and Farhad. Mirza Hadi Ruswa, the author of *Umrao Jan Ada*, was a modern Victorian scholar, a mathematician who lectured at Christian College, Lucknow. There is a difference of more than a hundred years in the characters' attitudes, observations and social mores. The socio-political conditions had entirely changed.

John Beams in his *Memoirs of a Bengal Civilian* says :"In the evening a social meeting was held in the same pavilion where the chief European officers and their wives met and did their best to be civil to native chiefs, while nautch girls danced before them and sang native songs through their noses..." The attitude had distinctly changed in a hundred years for the Europeans seeing a nautch (in this case probably an Odissi) was no more like "going to the ballet in Europe."

Let's go back to Hasan Shah's times. The life of luxury

lived by Ming and his colleagues portrayed in *Nashtar* was one side of the coin. The sack of Delhi by Abdali (1757) was followed by a long spell of what is known as John Company's period of loot. There were civil wars and general lawlessness (but mind you, never a single Hindu-Muslim riot!). Three major poets of Urdu—Mirza Rafi Sauda, Mir Taqi Mir and Nazir Akbarabadi, gave eyewitness accounts of the times in their long poems called *shehr ashob* (which would roughly mean disintegeration or destruction of a society, or city). In his famous *shehr ashob* Sauda (d. 1781) writes:

> Said I to Sauda the other day,
> Why do you dilly-dally so?
> Go, get a job, purchase a horse,
> Do something man, for goodness'
>   sake,
> Thereupon he laughed and said,
> Really!
> Pray tell me: Are they selling jobs
> in the market-place of Delhi-town?
> The barons bold are lying low,
> Their lands are gone, the rebels rule,
> The mighty lord of two-and-
>   twenty realms of Ind
> Hath not even the fief of Ko'l![1]
> All nobles, grandees, feudal
>   chiefs
> Have pawn'd their swords at bania shops,
> And roam the earth with begging-bowls.
> Thus what I mean, my honor'd friend,
> Such destitutes as you and I
> Should emigrate to Isfahan
> (Or seek some work in Istamboul!)
> A thousand homes are dark as no lamps burn,
> Owls hoot

---

1. Modern Aligarh.

Where once they sang
Hindola Rag in summer-
                  time;
Who blasted this Eden
one does not know—
The cursed one who
        stepped this way.
Cacti grow in cypress
                groves
Love birds have gone
and crows move in.
Jehanabad[1]—did'st thou
deserve this fate
That thou be crushed
        like a lover's heart?
Thou fairest shore on
        the sea of life
Whose sand gave pearls
        to the world at large!
Gentle dames of exalted birth
Have wrapped themselves
        from head to toe,
With bonny babies in their arms
They wander round from
door to door
Crying: "Rosaries of holy clay for sale!"
Ah my friend, I've
seen it all,
And if I get some peace
of mind
I shall sit down
and weep so
much
The citizens of Delhi-town
would drain their homes
O' my flood of tears.

---

1. Delhi.

Sauda, be still, it breaks my
                        heart,
There is such grief and
        pain to bear,
Weep no more, poor woeful man,
The times are bad,
We'd better be quiet .[1]

To employ famous musicians, both men and women, in their durbars was a status symbol for Indian princes. The performing artistes accompanied them on their masters' hunting trips as well as military campaigns. Mir Taqi Mir, the Urdu poet, describes, with great anguish, the decadence of the times when, he says, in his *shehr ashob* that "next-door to the lofty royal camp there stands the scarlet womens' camp. Licentiousness and drinking go on unabated. In short, the potentate is degenerate."

There was a reaction. It appeared in the form of a religious movement started by Shah Wali Ullah[2] (1703-1763).

Even *dargahs* had become places where nautch girls pitched their tents and held their dancing sessions. The new reformers became anti-music, more or less in the tradition of Aurangzeb. A few years earlier, after the death of Aurangzeb, as a reaction to his austere puritanism, Mohammed Shah Rangile (1719-1748) had made Delhi the musical capital of the East. The institution of *mujras* and *tawaifs* had come into being. Many of the courtesans came from Punjab, Rajasthan and Kashmir. The Nawab-Viziers of Oudh had appeared on the chessboard of 18th-century India as powerful military leaders. In the words of Maulana Abdul Halim Sharar, famous Urdu novelist and historian, the English actively encouraged the later kings of Oudh to become addicted to wine and women.

---

1. Abridged and translated by Q. Hyder.
2. Please see notes.

Therefore, in his view, the British themselves became part of the decadent scene only as long as it suited them.

Nevertheless, despite the emergence of the puritans, the Twilight of the Mughals coincided with the Renainssance at Delhi and Lucknow. The culture of the Kingdom of Oudh continues to flourish to some extent, till this day. Thus the characters of both *Nashtar* and *Umrao Jan Ada* assume greater significance for the modern reader as they afford a glimpse of the reality of the past. Hasan Shah's friendship with his boss Ming verifies the account of 'the Moonshie' as given in Hobson-Jobson which says that often "a lasting friendship was formed between the pupil and the Moonshee." At the same time Hasan Shah's helpless bondage to his foreign master is revealed in the final pages when Ming does not let his clerk go on leave because he must wind up his work first.

A tombstone stands in an English graveyard in Gola Gunj, Lucknow. It is popularly called Kallan-ki-Lat. It could have been the Kallan Saheb of our novel.

> IN MEMORY
> OF
> COLONEL JOHN COLLINS
> RESIDENT AT THE COURT OF
> LUCKNOW--1806-7
> DIED 11TH JUNE, 1807

The English had set up their earliest cantonment somewhere nearby. Hasan Shah says that when Khanum Jan and her family arrived from Benares they stayed at Bhim-ka-Akhara near the cantonment. As camp-followers they were wont to stay near military areas. The cemetery in which Khanum Jan was buried was also located near Bhim-ka-Akhara. Mir Taqi Mir, "the Lord of Poetry," was buried there in 1810.

Professor Spear mentions one Col. Collins who was Resident at the Scindia's court at Gawalior and was also known as King Collins in Bengal. Maybe he was the same Kallan Saheb who had been paymaster or Officer Commanding at Cawnpore during the 1780's.

Many Indian miniatures depict the sixteen adornments mentioned in this novel by Hasan Shah. The miniatures show a lady looking into a mirror while her maids attend to her in various stages of her make-up. The "sixteen adornments" comprised the following:

1. Perfumed bath.
2. Smoking the hair with fragrant incense.
3. Thick garlands of jasmine worn in the hair.
4. Threading pearls with strands of hair.
5. Making various kinds of hair braids and tying them with gold and silver ribbons.
6. Sprinkling of hair with silver dust *(afshan)* among Muslims and the use of *sindoor* among the Hindus to indicate the lady's married state.
7. Perfume.
8. White face powder *(ghaza)*.
9. Beauty spot.
10. *Lakha* to redden the lips.
11. *Kajal* or lamp-black as eyeliner.
12. *Missi*—black paste to give the gums a purple hue.
13. Jewellery and glass bangles.
14. Henna for nails, palms and soles.
15. *Paan* (betel leaf) whose juice reddened the lips.
16. *Arsi*—mirror-ring worn on the thumb to check one's make-up from time to time.

Khanum Jan had reached the stage of blackening her gums with *missi* when Hasan Shah arrived on the scene in chapter 6.

Among the novel's characters Mirzai and her relatives attract our attention. They are a deeply religious lot. They say their prayers five times a day and observe other rites of faith. And yet they are utterly amoral. Like most Indians they believe that they are only fulfilling their destiny! It had been pre-ordained that they be born as procurers and courtesans. Khanum Jan thinks differently and tries desperately to get out of that particular kind of caste-system.

An English visitor to the court of King Nasiruddin Hyder of Lucknow described a courtesan in the following words: "She had come form Punjab and she sang extremely well—The king sometimes made her wear European dress. She had a strange melancholy and shyness in her eyes." The description reminds one of Khanum Jan.

Among the characters, Khanum Jan emerges as the strongest. She has an extraordinary personality. Compared to her, Hasan Shah, the hero-narrator, is weak, dithering, and at times even comical. The Urdu translator makes funny comments about Hasan Shah's attitudes and behaviour. He is a callow youth often admonished by a very mature woman who is also slightly older than him. The Englishman, Ming, has come from Georgian England. He appreciates an educated and witty Khanum Jan who is an interesting conversationalist. Khanum Jan makes *Nashtar* remarkable both as a human document and a fascinating piece of literature.

Q.H.

Notes

1. Asaf-ud-Daulah (1775-1797), the 4th Nawab-Vizier of Oudh. After the death of Aurangzeb in 1707, the Mughal Empire disintegrated rapidly. The viceroys became independent rulers of their provinces. Of these the viceroys of Hyderabad Deccan, and Bengal-Bihar-Orissa, and Oudh, were powerful military leaders. The Nawab-Vizier of Oudh Asaf-du-Daulah, and Asaf Jah of Deccan were given the title of "Asaf", implying that these Ministers were as glorious as Asaf, the Vizier of King Solomon. Deccan's Asaf Jah was a heriditary title. (The last Asaf Jah, the Nizam of Hyderabad, was deposed in 1949, and his dominions were merged in the Republic of India.)
2. King Nasiruddin Hyder, 8th Ruler of Oudh (1827-1837). In order to further belittle the already vanquished Mughal Emperor of Delhi, the Government of the Hon'ble East India Company bestowed the title of "His Majesty the King" on Ghaziuddin Hyder (1814-1827), the 7th ruler of Oudh. King Nasiruddin Hyder was his son. The Kingdom of Oudh came to an end in 1857 and the last King, Vajid Ali Shah was exiled to Calcutta.
3. Mohammed Shah (1717-1739), one of the "Lesser Mughals" who was called Rangile (the Merry Monarch). It was during his colourful regime that Nadir Shah, the Warlord of Iran ,sacked Delhi in 1739 and carried away the Peacock Throne to his country. 1739 became a watershed in Indian history and came to signify the destruction of Delhi.
4. Raja Ram Narain "Mauzoon", Deputy Governor, or Naib Nazim of Bengal, Bihar and Orissa, in Nawab Sirajud Daulah's Government. He was a trusted and loyal friend of the young Nawab and played an important role in the statecraft of those troubled times. He was also a noted poet of Urdu and Persian. "Mauzoon" was his pen-name.

Siraj-ud-Daulah was killed after the fateful Battle of Plassey in 1757. When the tragic news was conveyed to the Raja he uttered spontaneously:

Ghazalan tum to waqif ho, kaho Majnun ke marney ki.
Diwana mar gaya aakhir ko, veeraney pey kya guzri.

After which he tore up his garment and ran away towards the woods.

Gazelles of the desert! you know how Majnu died! What happened to the wilderness after the crazed lover eventually vanished?

It is said that the Raja gave up the world and took sannyas. His famous couplet has come to mean the death of an idealist for a just cause.

5. Emperor Farrukh Siyar (1713-1719) was one of the weaker Mughals who presided over the dissolution of the empire.
6. Charles D'Oyley, (whose painting is reproduced on the dust jacket) was himself the son of a famous East India Company "nabob". He was born in Calcutta in 1781 and joined the Company's service in 1798. He was Opium Agent at Patna and was posted to Dacca from 1808 to 1828. His paintings include "The Dancing Women of Bengal" and "A Dancing Woman of Lucknow". Many British artists portrayed the contemporary social scene, especially of Asaf-ud-Dowla's Faizabad and Lucknow. Telly Kettle painted "Col. Poliers Watching a Nautch" and "A Dancing Girl" in Faizabad in 1772. The portrait of "the bibi of Charles Wombell" was done by Charles Smith in Lucknow in 1785. "A European and His Family" which shows the gentleman with his Indian wife and children, was painted at Lucknow by Francesco Renaldi in 1795. Then we have the portraits of "Jemdaani, bibi of William Hicky" by Thomas Hicky (Calcutta, 1792) and "Amber Kaur, bibi of Sir Charles Malet", by James Wales (1792). Thomas Hicky painted three devdasis of South India in 1805. There also exists the portrait of a stunningly beautiful lady of Faizabad sitting on a divan with the regal poise and grandeur of a begum. She was the "bibi" of a high-ranking English official.
(Ref: *British Portraiture in India* by Mildred Archer; courtesy: Yasmin Shahid Husain, London).

About a picture included in *Glimpses of World History* (p. 265) Professor Arnold Toynbee writes: "British administration in India, until the end of the eighteenth century, was in the hands of the East India Company's commercial officers, who would spend their entire working life abroad in its service. Their total isolation from England, before the era of steam transport, plunged them far more deeply into Indian life and culture than their nineteenth-century successors, members of a professional colonial administration who preserved a civil servant's aloofness from 'native' life. This absorption into the local culture—often slightingly referred to as 'going native'—is illustrated in an Indian print of 1800, which shows a British Resident, dressed in Indian clothing and smoking a hookah, entertaining himself at home with a nautch, or Indian dancing display."
7. Bibi is a Turki-Persian word used for a lady. In the days of the John Company it was downgraded to denote the unofficial wives (mostly courtesans) of Englishmen. When Englishwomen began to arrive in India in larger numbers, the custom of maintaining Indian mistresses was discontinued. Englishwomen

came to be called *burra bibi* (great ladies). The later "Mem Saheb" was the Indianised form of "Ma'm". Bibi, however, continues to be used as a term of respect for women in north India.

Many famous Englishmen married into noble families and their descendants formed a Eurasian aristocracy in north India.

Indian artists of "the Company School" also made drawings of dance bands of the kind described in Hasan Shah's novel. In one such group of Delhi (early 19th century), the names are inscribed in Urdu above each figure: Hyder Bakhsh Tawaif. Ata, herald of the tawaifs (this indicates that their manager ceremoniously announced the entry of famous performers on the concert floor), Roshana nayaka (madam), Kandu Kodak (a lad who reminds one of Hasan Shah's young Rahmullah). Another Delhi picture carries the following names: "Malagir Tawaif, favourite of Akbar Shah II; Umda; mother of Sehna; Chhote and Diljan tawaifs. Jaggu Khan nayak, Ali Bakhsh dhari, Qalandar Bakhsh and Khairati dhari (Dhari was a caste of professional musicians). The Persian caption says: Malagiri is dancing. She is a trainee of Meer Madari.

The men in these pictures stand around with their sarangis and tabla-bayan tied to their waists.

8. Nautch is a Hindustani word for dance. Kathak is north India's classical dance which had its old centres at Varanasi and Lucknow. It depicted the mystical romance of Radha and Krishna. Both Kathak and Rahas received tremendous encouragement and patronage from the Nawab-Viziers of Oudh. Kathak was danced by men as well as women. Maulana Abdul Halim Sharar, the social historian, reports that the masters of Kathak were mostly men and that there were two groups of dancers in Lucknow—Hindu Kathaks and *rahasdharies* and Kashmiri Muslim *bhands*. Among the former the best dancer was Khushi Maharaj of the Courts of Shuja-ud-Dowlah and Asaf-ud-Dowlah. During the reigns of the later kings of Oudh, Halaji, Prakashji and Diyaluji became famous dancers. Prakashji's son Durga Prashad is known to have taught the Kathak to the last King, Vajid Ali Shah. Durga Prashad's sons Kalka and Binda Din have become legendary. Their direct descendants include such masters of our own times as Shambhu Maharaj, Achchan Maharaj, Lachhoo Maharaj and Birju Maharaj. They have received international acclaim.

Kathak is no longer associated with the dancing girls. It is one of the most intricate and taxing dance forms. A number of highly educated women of the best families of India have become renowned exponents of this vigorous as well as lyrical dance style.

9. Deraydar tawaifs: The descendants of "tent-owners" are still called "deraydars" and were supposed to be the most eminent class of tawaifs. They had their own caste-rules. An interesting incident concerns Gohar Jan of Calcutta, the Eurasian prima donna of Urdu stage (d. 1932). Her own mother Malika Jan was a courtesan, and a metaphysical Urdu poet of repute! Other classy tawaifs did not treat Gohar as their peer because she was not of deraydar stock. Her mother was an Armenian and her father was probably a British or European Jew. When she went to Lucknow to learn Kathak from Kalka-Binda Din, she requested "the Chowdharain", one of the two formidable sisters called Nanwa-Bachwa, to induct her, through a special ceremony, as an honorary deraydar!

    Gohar Jan was a linguist and sang in seven different European and Indian languages. She was a politically conscious person and attended the early sessions of the Indian National Congress, till the ladies of Calcutta protested against the presence of a tawaif at the meetings. She danced with the Duke of Connaught but defied the Viceroy of India in a famous incident when she was barred from riding her coach-and-four (Indians were not allowed this privilege).

    Tagore did not allow anybody to tamper with his Rabindra Sangeet. Gohar merrily sang Tagore songs set to her own tunes and the poet graciously condoned her defiance.
10. Both Hafiz Shirazi (1325-1388) and Naziri belonged to Iran.
11. Maulana Jalaluddin Rumi or the Maulana of Rome (1207-1273) is one of the greatest mystic poets of the world. "Rumi" needs to be explained: after 330 A.D. Emperor Constantine moved his capital from Rome to Byzantium and called the city Constantinople, and "Second Rome". After the Turkish conquest, Turkey came to be known as Rome because it was the successor state of the Eastern Roman Empire. Therefore Maulana Jalaluddin was called "Rumi", and "Maulana Rome" (pronounced Room). In the Islamic world the Turkish Caliphs were also referred to as the Caliphs or Sultans of Rome, till the Ottoman Empire fell in 1919.

    Maulana Rumi's famous Whirling Dervishes have the headquarters of their Sufi Order at Konya, Turkey, where Rumi's mausoleum is situated.
12. Shah Waliullah of Delhi (1703-1762), was an outstanding metaphysician and philosopher. He belonged to the scholastic Naqshbandi School of mysticism. He was also against feudalism and preceded Karl Marx by almost a century when he propounded his theories of labour and capital. His grandson Shah Ismail started the movement of "Back to Pure Islam". By

that time many dargahs or sufi shrines had become centres of corruption. The nautch girls pitched their tents near dargahs during the saints' annual fairs. The reformers decried Sufism in its debased form, as it also encouraged superstition and indolence. Arabia's puritan leader Abdul Wahab (d. 1792) inspired Shah Ismail's movement of social and religious reform. The followers were called Wahabis. They also waged a relentless war against the British in India. They continued their warfare even after 1857. A large number of Wahabis were hanged by the British government. The present-day Sunni fundamentalists are the spiritual descendants of those early Wahabis.

13. Hussain Shah "Haqiqat" 's eldest son Syed Mohammed Hussain studied agriculture and engineering in London and wrote many books on agriculture. Hussain Shah's second son Mir Mohsin Lucknawi became a well-known poet. Mohsin Lucknawi's son Khan Bahadur Jaffer Hussain (d. 1936) and grandson Syed Hamid Hussain (d. 1945) were celebrated irrigation engineers of U.P. Other descendants of Hussain Shah include the late Syed Rafique Hussain, the unusual writer of animal stories, Altaf Fatima, the novelist, and Maj. General Shahid Hamid. Zafar Umar, the legendary police officer and the first writer of spy stories in Urdu was Syed Jaffer Hussain's son-in-law.
(Ref. *Hussain Shah Haqiqat and His Family* by Musharraf Ahmed; *courtesy:* Mushfique Khwaja, Karachi.)